The Power of Prayer

BY FRED R. BROCK, JR.

This book has been prepared primarily for group study in connection with the Adult Teacher's Guide available for 60¢ from Regular Baptist Press. However, it is also an excellent and informative book to use for individual instruction and to put into the hands of friends and acquaintances.

Published
by

REGULAR BAPTIST PRESS

1800 Oakton Boulevard

Des Plaines, Illinois 60018

CONTENTS

FOREWORD . . . . IFC

Chapters

1. Prayer and the Will of God 1

2. Kinds of Prayer 8

3. The Secret of Prayer 17

4. The Laws of Prayer 26

5. Reasons for Prayer 35

6. Hindrances to Prayer 44

7. Problems (Part I) 54

8. Problems (Part II) 62

9. A Study of Jesus' Prayer Life 71

10. Powerful Pray-ers 80

11. Prayer—Worry—Healing 89

12. How To Pray 98

13. Promises! Promises! Promises! 108

14. The Lord's Prayer 117

Copyright 1975 by Regular Baptist Press. Vol. 23, No. 4. Printed in U.S.A. Dr. Merle R. Hull, Executive Editor; Ruth Herriman, Managing Editor.

CHAPTER 1

Prayer and the Will of God

BIBLE PORTION TO READ: Romans 8:1-27

A STUDY OF PRAYER cannot be expected to turn up anything new, much less original. In a series of this sort, the intention is not to be technical or even theological but, hopefully, practical. There is no need to prove the fact of prayer or the need for prayer; but there is a need to encourage the practice of prayer.

Andrew Murray, the great Scottish preacher of a past generation (1828-1917), has written, The "power of prayer in the Christian life is too little understood. . . . As long as we look on prayer chiefly as the means of maintaining our own Christian life [asking for things], we shall not know fully what it is meant to be. But when we learn to regard it as the highest part of the work entrusted to us [Eph. 2:10], the root and strength of all other work, we shall see that there is nothing that we so need to study and practise as the art of praying aright."

We again quote Andrew Murray: "The Father waits to hear every prayer of faith, to give us whatsoever we will, and whatsoever we ask in Jesus' name. We have become so accustomed to limit the wonderful love and the large promises of our God, that we cannot read the simplest and clearest statements of our Lord without the qualifying clauses by which we guard and expound them. If there is one thing . . . the Church needs to learn, it is that God means prayer to have an answer, and that it hath not entered into the heart of man to conceive what God will do for His child who gives himself to believe that his prayer will be heard."

The most powerful thing a Christian can do is pray. Prayer is no childish prattle; neither is it the mumblings of the aged, the sick and the dying. Prayer is dynamic cooperation with God! When men pray, God acts! Nothing lies outside the reach and power of prayer except that which lies outside God's will.

Prayer is the greatest resource available to man. It lifts us out of the slough of despond to the hilltops of God where we drink in the vision of "all things possible" and breathe the heady atmosphere of communion with God. By prayer a common man becomes uncommon, for he moves Heaven and shakes Hell. Spurgeon said, "If a man can pray, he can do anything."

Prayer is not a burden to be borne but a gift to be enjoyed. It is not seeking favors from God but accepting orders from God. May we join the disciples as we come to these lessons saying, "Lord, teach us to pray!"

I. Prayer and the Will of God

We quote S. D. Gordon in his great work *Quiet Talks on Prayer,* in the chapter "Something about God's Will in Connection with Prayer": "The purpose of prayer is to get God's will done." And again, "The whole thought in prayer is to get the will of . . . God . . . done in our lives and upon this old earth. The greatest prayer any one can offer is, 'Thy will be done.' "

If this be true—and certainly it should be true—then God is indeed a stranger in His own world and must stand like a mendicant begging men to let Him into their hearts and lives so that He may show them His will and lead them in it. No one is more sorely neglected or sadly slandered than is God. We peer suspiciously at Him and His promises as though His will were hard, harsh, undesirable, unwanted, bitter and un-

A Verse To Memorize

"And he that searcheth the hearts knoweth what is the mind of the Spirit, because he maketh intercession for the saints according to the will of God" (Rom. 8:27).

pleasant. We act as though He was impish, niggardly, jealous, tyrannical and unkind for even asking us to do His will. Do we not believe that God's will is perfect, that His will is good? Do we not believe Matthew 7:11: "If ye then, being evil, know how to give good gifts unto your children, how much more shall your Father which is in heaven give good things to them that ask him"? Do we not believe John 15:15: "Henceforth I call you not servants; . . . I have called you friends"? Are we afraid of God's will? Is that why we are afraid to pray? Or why don't we?

In Romans 12:1 and 2 Paul promised that if we will yield ourselves completely to God, we will discover that His will is good, acceptable and perfect. Do we want to risk missing God's will? Are we afraid to pray, "Thy will be done"? Just a brief study of the above three words will dispel any fears we might have along this line.

A. The will of God is *good*. Three words in the New Testament are translated "good." The first is the word *cosmos* which comes into English in the word cosmetics. It means "orderly, properly arranged, adorned." Hence it means "good looking." The universe is referred to as the cosmos because it is an orderly arrangement. Secondly, we have the word *kalos* which is recognizable in the English word calisthenics. This word means "intrinsically good, goodly, fair, noble, honorable, wholesome and healthy." The third word has no English equivalent. Like the word *agape* (love), it is a qualitative word denoting moral, spiritual, quality, character. It is the word *agathos*. See Titus 2:5 where we have *agathos* translated "good." Note Titus

3

2:7 and 3:1 where we read *kalos* describing works—"good works"—and *agathos* describing work—"good work." In Titus 2:10 the word "adorn" is *cosmos*.

It is easy to see that when Paul used *agathos* in Romans 12:2, he was saying that God's will is the best kind of good there is. This is not a comparative term such as good, better and best; but it is a qualitative term guaranteeing to us who do God's will the very best thing possible.

B. The will of God is *acceptable*. This word, too, is descriptive. It is made up of the words "well" and "pleasing." In other words, God's will is guaranteed to be well pleasing. Usually we look askance at what we do not know or understand and hence are inclined to put it in an unfavorable light. All of us have discovered that a certain food we thought unpalatable, when we were children is indeed delicious now that we have tasted it. So it is with the will of God. Anyone, everyone who has yielded himself to God's Word and the leading of the Holy Spirit has found the will of God to be sweet, good and very well pleasing. Paul guarantees this. (Read Proverbs 3:5 and 6; Ephesians 5:10; Philippians 4:18 and Titus 2:9.)

C. Finally, Paul said, the will of God is *perfect*. Here the word means "finished, complete, mature, fulfilled." Anyone who has passed the age of sixty knows how many people that age have little to talk about except "what might have been." Life seems to have been full of hard work, missed opportunities and failures. But this was not so with Paul who could approach the end of life and say, "I have finished my course" (2 Tim. 4:7), and be happy about it. The satisfaction of knowing that one's life has been productive, effective and full is a source of real blessing and enjoyment rather than a series of struggles and disappointments. Such a blessed life is found in the will of God. Paul guarantees this fact! Prayer makes possible knowing it. Let us then pray for and in the will of God!

4

II. Two Wills of God?

When we pray, "Thy will be done," it is not to mean locking our jaws, gritting our teeth and saying, "Thy will be endured, whatever it is." Too many of us have the idea that everything in a Christian's life is to be understood as the will of God whether it be good, bad or in between. S. D. Gordon has commented: "It may help us here to remember that God has a first and a second will for us: a first choice and a second. He always prefers that His first will shall be accomplished in us. But where we will not be wooed up to that height, He comes down to the highest level we will come up to, and works with us there." Gordon illustrated this point by saying that it was not the will of God for Israel to have a human line of kings determined by royal succession since He chose and appointed all leaders. However, when Israel insisted (1 Sam. 8:1-9), God set up kings. The first of these was Saul who was displaced by David and his line. David himself wrote in Psalm 106:15: "And he gave them their request; but sent leanness into their soul." Notice further the well-known portion in John 21:15-17 where Jesus twice asked Peter, "Lovest thou me?" and used the greatest word for love *(agape)*. Twice Peter responded with a lesser word *(phileo)*. Then Jesus came down to Peter's word in His third querie, thus illustrating this second will of God.

This author feels that even though the above seems logically, perhaps Scripturally, to be true, yet it is a deviation from the rule and is therefore an irregularity. It seems that God can have only one will for men or a man since He is perfect. Perhaps Gordon modified his position when he said, "It may be said that God has two wills for each of us, or, better, there are two parts to His will." He referred to these two parts as "His will of grace, and His will of government." The first is plainly revealed in His Word. The second is His particular plan for my life (Eph. 2:10). In the first case, we need only "intelligent willingness." In the second we

5

need a yieldedness to the guidance indicated by the Holy Spirit and circumstances.

Three means of determining God's will seem to be relevant since all three must be bathed by prayer:

A. *The chance method, or Gideon's fleece.* We cannot deny that Gideon used a "fleece" to determine the will of God (Judg. 6:36-40). Neither can we deny that God honored his prayer. However, it should be noted that in Judges 6:16 God promised Gideon victory over the Midianites; and the next verse records that Gideon asked for a sign which God gave to him.

Did Gideon need anything more? Was the fleece necessary? Ought not Gideon have removed the question in verses 36-40, acting upon the directive already given? With the confirmation already given, shouldn't he have proceeded against Midian? We cannot say that Gideon was right or wrong, but it seems evident that he had his answer before he put out the fleece.

A grosser and more dangerous form of this kind of prayer is the "flip-the-coin" method: "Heads I do; tails I don't." Again we read, "The lot is cast into the lap; but the whole disposing thereof is of the LORD" (Prov. 16:33). This would seem to countenance such a practice, particularly after praying about it.

Wisdom would seem to suggest clearly that we seek the instruction of God's Word, the counsel of the Holy Spirit and that we bathe the matter in prayer. All of us know that having done all this, we still find occasions when we would need God to indicate His mind and will; therefore, we ask for a sign or put out a fleece. Never employ such a method and then renege. Never change the terms if the results are not what you hoped for. Psalm 15:4 tells us that "he that sweareth to his own hurt, and changeth not" is one of the characteristics of one who "abide[s] in thy tabernacle [and] . . . dwell[s] in thy holy hill" (Ps. 15:1). Even if the deal with God turned out wrong, you may not change. It is better to wait upon God, pray earnestly and then wait!

B. *Then there is the "thus saith the Lord" method*

which seems to need little comment because "If God says it, that settles it." If we prayerfully read and absorb God's Word, we will know and willingly yield to God's revealed will (Ps. 25:9): "The meek will he guide . . . the meek will he teach his way."

C. *Finally there is the leading of the Holy Spirit and circumstances.* Romans 8:26-28 seems to indicate clearly that the Holy Spirit, Who admittedly knows the mind and will of God better than any of us, will see to it that the "will of God" be known by each one of us in particular. The Holy Spirit teaches us to pray in God's will. He Himself prays God's will for us so that we will then reach up to where we ourselves know what the will of God is.

Let us, therefore, not pray by chance but according to God's Word which we have absorbed through daily meditation and under the discipline of the Holy Spirit and the suggestion of circumstances. Let us pray with boldness as in and because of 1 John 5:14 and 15.

Prepare To Discuss Intelligently

1. Illustrate the three kinds of "good" used in the Scriptures. Which one describes the will of God?

2. How does Paul describe the will of God in Romans 12:2?

3. What three methods for determining the will of God do we consider here?

4. Classify the above methods according to how important you feel they are.

Sources of Quotations

Gordon, S. D. "Something about God's Will in Connection with Prayer," *Quiet Talks on Prayer.* Old Tappan, NJ: Fleming H. Revell Co., 1904, pp. 177, 182, 183, 184, 187, 188. Used by permission.

Murray, Andrew. *With Christ in the School of Prayer.* Grand Rapids: Zondervan Publishing House, pp. 6, 7. Used by permission.

CHAPTER 2

Kinds of Prayer

BIBLE PORTIONS TO READ: Ephesians 6:10-20; 1
Timothy 2:1-4

THESE LESSONS are not an exposition of a portion
of Scripture; rather, they are an application of
Scripture. This lesson is not intended as a lesson in the
Greek language either to demonstrate the extensive
learning of the author or to discourage those who have
no access to or ability in the area. It is recognized that
word studies are poor vehicles for teaching doctrine
since no one word is likely to express all the truth in any
given area. However, word studies are very illustra-
tive and follow the injunction to "compare Scripture
with Scripture." Therefore, we do need to study the
meanings of words used in Scripture.

A suggestion, perhaps a distortion, concerning the
word "always" in Luke 18:1 might be that we hyphenate
the word in this way: "all-ways." The Lord Jesus
Christ is then made to say that men ought to pray all
kinds of ways. The reader may rest assured that the
term employed *(pantotes)* allows for such a rendering.
Hence a listing of the words in Scripture which are
translated "prayer" or very obviously mean prayer
would be proper and possibly helpful.

I. Words for Prayer

A. The word *euche* (pronounced you-kay) means "a wish." In James 5:15 we read, "And the prayer of faith shall save the sick." Second Corinthians 13:7 is rendered, "Now I pray to God that ye do no evil"; and verse 9 uses the same word to say, "This also we wish, even your perfection." To this author it seems that one who really walks with God prays like this much of the time. It certainly suggests a childlike confidence which may explain the reason for the frequent failure as given in James 5:15.

B. A compound of this word *proseuche* (pros-you-kay) means "prayer or wishing toward"; and it is always directed toward God. This is the "wish upon a star," or "star light, star bright" kind of prayer which, when directed to a star or four-leaf clover, is nothing more than a wish; but when directed toward God, it becomes a real prayer, the only real prayer. We see this in the following references: 1 Thessalonians 5:17; Matthew 21:22; Luke 6:12; James 5:17; Ephesians 6:18 and Philippians 4:6.

C. *Deesis* (dee-ay-sis) has the "asking with the emphasis on a need." The previous word means prayer in general while this one is specific and is also used of asking man to man. In Luke 1:13 we read, "Thy prayer is heard; and thy wife Elisabeth shall bear thee a son." The following references—Luke 2:37; Romans 10:1; 2 Corinthians 1:11; 9:14 and Philippians 1:4—use the word as "prayer" and "request." Philippians 1:4 reads, "Always in every prayer [*deesis*] of mine for you all making request [*deesis*] with joy." Also read Philippians 1:19; 2 Timothy 1:3 and 1 Peter 3:12, noting the ways the word is used.

D. *Erotao* (aero-taow) means to "make request." It is usually used as coming from one considered an equal and able to respond or from one with whom we are familiar. In Luke 14:18 we read, "I pray thee have me excused." John 4:31 reads, "His disciples prayed him, saying, Master, eat." In John 14:16 we read, "And

9

I will pray the Father, and he shall give you another Comforter." See also John 16:26 and 17:9, 15 and 20 for further illustration on this type of prayer.

E. *Aiteo* (eye-teh-o) means "to ask." As contrasted with the previous word, this word suggests a petition by one who is lesser than the one petitioned. Such is the case of the man asking from God in Matthew 7:7: "Ask, and it shall be given you." Verse 9 reads, "If his son ask bread, will he give him a stone?" In Ephesians 3:20 we see the remarkable promise: "Now unto him that is able to do exceeding abundantly above all that we ask or think." Another pertinent verse is Colossians 1:9. Note also James 1:5 and 6: "If any of you lack wisdom, let him ask of God, that giveth to all men liberally, and upbraideth not; and it shall be given him. But let him ask in faith, nothing wavering." James 4:2 and 3 read, "Ye have not, because ye ask not. Ye ask, and receive not, because ye ask amiss." (See also 1 John 3:22; 5:14, 15 and 16.) *Aiteo* comes from a root which means "one who crouches"; hence it indicates a humble asking.

F. Supplication comes from the work *hiketeria* (hick-tear-eeah) used only once—in Hebrews 5:7—although it occurs twice in the Greek version of the Old Testament—one of which is Job 41:3. This word very literally and graphically means "to bear an olive branch." In other words, the supplicant is so insistent and so persistent that he could expect a rebuke; but he is pleading to be heard because the burden upon his heart is so great.

G. Intercession is from the word *enteuxiss* (en-teuk-sis) which means "to meet to converse." According to

Vine's *Expository Dictionary*, it is a technical term "for approaching a king, and so for approaching God in intercession," in behalf of another! In Romans 8:26 we see it translated, "But the Spirit itself maketh intercession *[huperenteuksis]*." First Timothy 4:5 and 2:1 give another catalog of the kinds and varieties of prayer. Intercession is illustrated in John 17:15 and 17 although the word itself is not used. Such is the case in Luke 22:31 and 32 and Colossians 1:9ff.

H. The last word used is *entungchano* or *hyperentungchano*, and it signifies dialogue. The words listed in points G and H are similar in the sense of a meeting of two persons for conversation; but this last term emphasizes the aspect of pleading, not just conversation, and the petition in behalf of someone else. Romans 11:2 signifies dialogue "against." This is no less than negative intercession. In Romans 8:27 we read, "Because he maketh intercession *[entungchano]* for the saints." Verse 34 of the same chapter reads, "who also maketh intercession *[entungchano]* for us," thus recording the intercession of the Holy Spirit and of Christ our High Priest on our behalf. Again Romans 8:26 and Hebrews 7:25 emphasize the true nature of intercession. That we should be able to approach God at all is marvelous, but that we can come boldly and discuss with Him anyone or anything and plead God's mercy and grace in their behalf is a miracle. However, everything about prayer is indeed a miracle!

II. Prayer Defined by Function

There may be a problem in defining prayer by the words used since it presents the objective aspect designed by God to help people, but prayer is asking from God; and it is designed by God to help people. However, prayer is much more than getting things. Prayer is a relationship between people and their God.

A. *Prayer is adoration, worship, reverence, homage and fellowship.* It is not incidental that the prayer our Lord taught begins by saying, "Our Father which art in heaven" (Matt. 6:9). Prayer must begin with this recognition that we are entering into God's presence. There are no promises claimed, no list of requests, no pleading for needs—either ours or others—but just reveling in the presence of God. "Prayer is a spiritual experience," says Lindsell, "during which life's temporal realities fade, competing thoughts and fancies burn to ashes in the consuming presence of the Lord God. It is the summum bonum of spiritual reality."

Note such verses as 2 Kings 19:15 where Hezekiah prayed, "Oh LORD God of Israel, which dwellest between the cherubims, thou art the God, even thou alone, of all the kingdoms of the earth; thou hast made heaven and earth." Similarly, note the instance of 2 Chronicles 20:6 where Jehoshaphat was speaking.

Nowhere are worship and adoration presented more often or more clearly than in the Psalms. Read Psalm 29:2: "Give unto the LORD the glory due unto his name; worship the LORD in the beauty of holiness." Psalm 19:1 says that "the heavens declare the glory of God"; and Psalm 8:1 reads, "O LORD our Lord, how excellent is thy name in all the earth! who hast set thy glory above the heavens."

And in the New Testament the words of 1 Timothy 1:17 state, "Now unto the King eternal, immortal, invisible, the only wise God, be honour and glory for ever and ever." So, too, in Jude 25 it says, "To the only wise God our Saviour, be glory and majesty, dominion and power, both now and ever." (See also 2 Timothy 4:18.)

Such an attitude, such reverence and worship place one in the arms of God where prayer is as simple as breathing.

B. *Prayer Is Thanksgiving.* Like adoration, prayer with thanksgiving asks for nothing and hence is often neglected. Failure to thank God or the misuse of thanksgiving will inevitably result in impotence and atrophy. We must cultivate an "attitude of gratitude"

12

if we are to maintain our spiritual vitality. To be always asking and getting without returning thanks will produce a greedy, avaricious selfishness that will destroy our joy in prayer.

Thanksgiving is both negative and positive. It is praise to God for things avoided or from which we have been delivered, as well as for blessings bestowed. It is recorded that when John Wesley broke his arm, he thanked God that it was only his arm and not his head. Whether or not we pray for protection as we go out upon the highways, we should certainly thank God every time we drive into our garages that we have been spared accident or injury.

The Scriptures command thanksgiving. Psalm 50: 14 admonishes us to "offer unto God thanksgiving; and pay thy vows unto the most High." Verse 23 of the same chapter comments, "Whoso offereth praise glorifieth me: and to him that ordereth his conversation aright will I shew the salvation of God." Look up and read carefully Ephesians 5:20; Philippians 4:6; Colossians 4:2 and Revelation 7:12. Note, too, the disappointment in the healing of the lepers (Luke 17:11-19) as Jesus remarked, "Were there not ten cleansed? but where are the nine?" Only one (vv. 15, 16) returned to give thanks. Is it not noteworthy that Jesus' prayer at the tomb of Lazarus (John 11:41) began, "Father, I thank thee." So at the Last Supper "he took the cup, and when he had given thanks, he gave it to them" (Mark 14:23).

Cultivate the habit of remembering to give thanks. Someone has said, "Keep short accounts with God." It will pay rich dividends to make thanksgiving for the Person, presence and gifts of God in the opening paragraph of every prayer.

C. *Prayer Is Confession.* It must ever be remembered that prayer is the communion of sinners with a holy God. David wrote, "If I regard iniquity in my heart, the Lord will not hear me" (Ps. 66:18). Our salvation is not destroyed by sin, but communion and power in prayer may thus be broken. In 1 John 1:9 God has made clear that His desire is to cleanse sin in the experience of a believer as well as forgive sin in a repentant sinner. He has obligated Himself to "forgive us our sins, and to cleanse us from all unrighteousness."

The parable of the publican and the Pharisee in Luke 18:9-14 forever illustrates the proper attitude; namely, prayer made holy by confession. A study of Judas' remorse (Matt. 27:3-5) and of the rich man and Lazarus (Luke 16:19-31) compared with the thief at Calvary (Luke 23:39-43) may be helpful in illustrating the difference between repentance and remorse and between confession which works and confession that fails. The Prodigal in Luke 15 reinforces this matter of real and superficial confession.

One needs to be careful that he does not impugn God's mercy and grace by dwelling in masochistic contemplation upon the decayed and often disinterred corpses of past sins. Sins that are confessed are forgiven; and although we may not remove the scars, we should look upon them as the evidence of the healing of a wound or a disease and not repeatedly reopen them. David's experience in 2 Samuel 12, especially verse 13 followed by verses 14-23, is adequate illustration.

In this same area it may be well to think a moment about "sins of omission." We recall James's words in 4:17 of his Epistle: "Therefore, to him that knoweth to do good, and doeth it not, to him it is sin." John similarly enjoined (1 John 3:16-22) that since our lovely Lord laid down His life for us, we ought to do as much for the brethren. Further, if we see a brother have need but do nothing or—worse yet—shut up our compassion, we are in trouble.

Again we are reminded that if we "love in word," but fail to love in deeds and genuinely, our hearts should "condemn us." Only when our hearts "condemn us not" do we come to God with confidence in prayer. In other words, our failures and our omissions may effectively hinder our prayer lives. Confession would be a logical remedy and a necessary aspect of effectual prayer.

D. *Prayer Is Petition.* All of us have seen the little plaque "J-esus, O-thers, Y-ou." In other words, J-O-Y spells joy. The same is especially true in prayer. Adoration, thanksgiving and confession are kinds of prayer, but the major kind of prayer for all of us is petition. All of us should already have memorized Jeremiah 33:3: "Call unto me, and I will answer thee, and shew thee great and mighty things, which thou knowest not." There is nothing in all of God's Word which discourages us to come to God boldly and petition Him for our needs and those of others. A proper order in prayer, however, would be prayer for what God desires, then for the needs of others and finally for ourselves—that is the J-O-Y formula.

If our treatment of this form of prayer seems brief, it is not unintentional. The first reason for this is because we have no problem in understanding and practicing this kind of prayer; the second is because we do not need to support the possible overemphasis. We tend to judge almost everything by results, and the observable results from petition exceed those from prior forms. We hope only to urge balance rather than great emphasis on petition. Let us never forget that "whatsoever ye ask" is a frequently repeated encouragement; and "abundantly above" is the promise God gives to those who ask. (Reread Matthew 21:22; John 11:22; 14:13; 15:16; 16:23 and Ephesians 3:20 for further emphasis.)

E. *Prayer Is Intercession.* Petition is thought of as making requests for ourselves and our own needs or wants. As distinguished from this, we think of intercession as prayer *for* or *in behalf of* others and their needs. If we can meet or help meet the needs of others, we should do so; but if we need help in order that we may give help, we intercede. Those for whom we pray may or may not know their need or desire our help;

15

but as we understand the will of God, our hearts are burdened to pray for them.

Note the Biblical examples of intercession in the lives of Abraham (Gen. 18:23-33), Moses (Exod. 32: 11-14, 30-35) and Joshua (Josh. 7:7-9). Then note our Lord's intercession for the people before the cross (Luke 23:34); for the disciples (John 17:15, 17) and for Peter (Luke 22:31, 32). See also Paul's intercession for the churches (Col. 1:9) and his admonition to Timothy to pray "for all men" (1 Tim. 2:1).

May God help us to meditate upon the enormous potential we have in prayer and to use it to the full. May He help us to classify our prayers and apply to them consciously that form or kind of prayer which is likely to work best. Truly, Lord, teach us to pray "all ways."

Prepare To Discuss Intelligently

1. What is the main difference between prayers of petition and those of intercession?

2. What is the main difference between *erotao* and *aiteo*?

3. What meaning in the root of the word suggests this latter definition?

4. How many kinds of prayer can you list without using the text?

5. Name the five functions of prayer.

Source of Quotations

Lindsell, Harold. "Kinds of Prayer," *When You Pray*. Wheaton, IL: Tyndale House Publishers, Inc., 1969, pp. 30, 31, 34, 37, 39, 44, 49. Used by permission.

CHAPTER 3

The Secret of Prayer

BIBLE PORTION TO READ: John 15:1-20

"BELIEF IN PRAYER is a far cry from effectiveness in prayer" (*When You Pray*, Lindsell, p. 5). Many of those who pray more often and much longer than Christians normally do are hopelessly caught up in a ritual which lacks life, satisfaction or power. Many who call themselves Christians are better characterized by Jesus' remark concerning "vain repetitions" (Matt. 6:7).

All men direct their prayers to God or to a god. They also recognize that they have an obligation to pray as well as desiring the advantages and benefits that prayer is intended to produce. Surely there must be more of a secret to this matter than that "every man pray to his own god in his own way" as was suggested at the beginning of the opening session of the United Nations in San Francisco in 1945. Every nation represented and every religion was asked to pray in this way during a period of silent prayer. Surely prayer is more than a "psychological assist" as has been declared by the naturalist, the humanist and most psychiatrists.

In order to be real, prayer must be properly addressed—not to "a god" or to "any god"—but to the one true God. Otherwise, as is stated in Psalm 135:15-18 and Psalm 115:1-18, prayer is to gods whose eyes see not, whose ears hear not and whose mouths and hands are helpless. Read the requirements God sets forth in Hebrews 11:6 and John 14:6.

Note also the statements in Deuteronomy 6:4 and Isaiah 44:6 and 8.

If, then, we recognize the uniqueness of God and the requirement of approach to God through Jesus Christ, we are in a fair way to discern the secret of successful prayer.

I. The Secret of Prayer Is Abiding

"Abiding" seems to be set forth as the main—if not the sole—secret of prayer and fruitfulness. Not less than eleven words are used in the New Testament to express and define this word "abide." Each of these words is used in connection with prayer. An examination of these words should prove helpful to those who seek the secret of effectual prayer.

A. *Meno* (men-oh) which is translated abide, continue and dwell (1 John 2:17; 1 Cor. 13:13; 1 Pet. 1:23). There is also a whole series of compounds in which the verb is coupled with a preposition to enhance the meaning and force of the word:

1. *Epimeno* (epee-men-oh) meaning continue as it is translated in 1 Timothy 4:16.

2. *Katameno* (kahtah-men-oh) means constancy or frequency as it is used in 1 Corinthians 16:6.

3. *Parameno* (pahorah-men-oh) has the meaning of proximity. See Philippians 1:25 for this use.

4. *Hupomeno* (who-pah-men-oh), as used in Matthew 10:22, is translated "endureth."

5. *Prosmeno* (praas-men-oh) means to cling to a person or thing. We have it used in this way in Matthew 15:32.

B. *Diatribo* (dee-ah-tree-bow) is another word used and means to remain in contact. It is composed of two words (*dia*—through) and (*tribo*—rub). Read Acts 14:3 to see its use.

18

C. *Aulizomai* (ow-lee-zo-mai) has the meaning of lodging or camping outdoors. Verses where it is used are: Luke 21:37 and Matthew 21:17. Also see the next word.

D. *Agrauleo* (ah-graw-lee-oo) means to lodge in a barn, shelter or fold. It is used in Luke 2:8: "And there were in the same country shepherds abiding in the field, keeping watch over their flock by night."

E. *Histemi* (hiss-tay-me) has the meaning of to stand or remain in position. Note its use regarding Satan in John 8:44: "Ye are of your father the devil, and the lusts of your father ye will do. He was a murderer from the beginning, and abode not in the truth, because there is no truth in him. When he speaketh a lie, he speaketh of his own: for he is a liar, and the father of it."

F. *Poieo* (poy-ey-oh) means to make or spend time. We find it used in Acts 15:33 ("And after they had tarried there a space, they were let go in peace from the brethren unto the apostles") and 2 Corinthians 11:25 ("Thrice was I beaten with rods, once was I stoned, thrice I suffered shipwreck, a night and a day have I been in the deep").

Jesus did not use any of the compound words, but simply the word *meno*. There is no big dark secret about abiding. It simply means to remain where you are—"in Christ." As Israel was commanded to do in Deuteronomy 6:5 and 6, we are simply to love the Lord Jesus Christ with all our hearts, minds and souls. In this way we are to be abiding. There is really nothing complex about abiding; it is "simply trusting every day."

The Scofield Reference Bible (old edition) has a

19

note on John 15:4 that is worth repeating: "Abide in me, and I in you. As the branch cannot bear fruit of itself, except it abide in the vine; no more can ye, except ye abide in me." To this Scofield added: "To abide in Christ is, on the one hand, to have no known sin unjudged and unconfessed, no interest into which He is not brought, no life which He cannot share. On the other hand, the abiding one takes all burdens to Him, and draws all wisdom, life and strength from Him. It is not unceasing consciousness of these things, and of Him, but that nothing is allowed in the life which separates from Him."

II. The Secret of Prayer Is Believing Faith

Another way of expressing this truth that in Christ we simply "trust and obey," thus resulting in an effective prayer life, is in the word "believe." Our attitude toward God in the matter of prayer must be one of believing. We repeat the opening quotation: "Belief in prayer is a far cry from effectiveness in prayer." "The potential of prayer is jeopardized because so few of those who say they believe in prayer speak from personal and continued experience in prayer."

Several premises must be established, one of which is: *God answers prayer.* Do we believe that? If He doesn't, we need go no further. If He does, then prayer is the most serious business in which we can engage. When we read Jeremiah 33:3, God plainly states that He will "shew thee great and mighty things, which thou knowest not."

In Matthew 7:7 and 8 Jesus similarly affirms that if we ask, seek and knock, He will answer. The testimony of thousands is that God answers prayer. Read Psalm 34:8 and Malachi 3:10. Many would gladly testify to the truth of the phrase, "Prayer changes things," by asserting that "prayer changes men" and it has changed them. No amount of argument is guaranteed to persuade an unbeliever. But no amount of unbelief should deter a believer from proving the viability of prayer based on the promise that God will answer. We know this because, like David, we called and God did answer us. Note the following references from the Book of Psalms: 6:9; 34:4 and 116:1 and 2.

Our union with Christ, like the union of the branch and the vine, is one of never-ceasing growth and increase. This abiding not only produces growth in grace and knowledge, but it also produces growth in faith and experience. As feeding upon the Word of God produces increase of knowledge and growth in grace, so believing prayer produces a wealth of experience which confirms the existence of God and the validity of prayer to God.

III. The Secret of Prayer Is Obeying

Andrew Murray, in his book *With Christ in the School of Prayer,* has written: "Obedience and faith must go together. Not as if to the faith he has the obedience must be added, but faith must be made manifest in obedience. Faith is obedience at home [inward, subjective] and looking to the Master. Obedience is faith [outward, objective] going out to do His will."

"If ye keep my commandments, ye shall abide in my love," said Jesus in John 15:10; and one of those commandments is, "Pray without ceasing" (1 Thess. 5: 17).

Prayer is an obligation to Christians. Martin Luther wrote, "As it is the business of tailors to make clothes and cobblers to mend shoes, so it is the business of Christians to pray."

Read *Prayer Explained* by W. A. Pritchard, page 9. Also meditate on Luke 18:1; 1 Thessalonians 5:17; Philippians 4:6; 1 Timothy 2:1 and Ephesians 6:18 and 19.

Recognizing this obligation to pray, Samuel said, "Moreover as for me, God forbid that I should sin against the LORD in ceasing to pray for you." How great must be the culpability of many who fail to pray, who even promise to pray and do not do so. If a nurse is assigned the responsibility to give medicine to a patient, but instead she becomes interested in something else so that she fails to administer the medication, she may be criminally negligent. Could the same be true of our failure to do the business of Christians as Luther has remarked!

IV. The Secret of Prayer Is Believing It Is Necessary

It has been said that "we cannot suppose that God will do for us *without* prayer what He has promised to do for us only *through* prayer." Not only did Jesus command, "Watch ye therefore, and pray always [always?]" (Luke 21:36); but Paul enjoined, "Pray without ceasing" (1 Thess. 5:17). Peter exhorted us, "Watch unto prayer" (1 Pet. 4:7).

We quote Lindsell again: "Prayer is necessary because its absence is the surest means of cutting oneself off from God, permitting the spiritual life to wither. Prayerlessness produces sterility of spiritual perception, a life without holiness and a witness without power" (p. 21). Read Mark 9:29.

Not only is prayer necessary because God commands it, but it is also necessary because we need it. Do we believe that?

It is almost trite to suggest that activity has become the substitute for prayer, meditation, devotional reading, etc. Similarly, organization has become a replacement for consecration. Planning, programming and promotion have taken the place of praying in the life of the average church and Christian. Doesn't the experience of Mary and Martha in Luke 10:38-42 become a proper rebuke to us who allow ourselves to be "cumbered about much serving," a great part of which has no value spiritually, but it keeps us too busy to pray?

E. M. Bounds, in his little book *Power Through Prayer*, has remarked: "Men are God's method. The Church is looking for better methods; God is looking for better men." History makes clear that when men prayed, revivals were born and miracles were spawned.

22

Conversely, the church slowed and slumped even though activity and machinery were added. This makes plain the vital importance of prayer.

Note 2 Chronicles 20:12-25 where King Jehoshaphat overcame an invading army by prayer. The command of God was to get ready but to trust God to answer prayer (vv. 16, 17); and the victory came because a king whose business it was to fight wars believed he had bigger business with greater promise of success by prayer.

Second Kings 19:14-37 records the prayer of Hezekiah and the ignominious defeat of Sennacherib as a direct result. The next chapter (20:1-11) records the miraculous restoration of Hezekiah from a mortal illness and the extension of his life by fifteen years. However, it did not prevent stupidity in another instance (20:12 and 19); and an extension of life in one case does not mean a repeat performance of blessing (20:20, 21).

All of this simply emphasizes our obligation to pray. Unless we see prayer as absolutely necessary and commanded to be done, we will not pray; then we will wonder why nothing happens. Or else we will increase our activity and begin quoting numbers in proof of success (?) in spite of our failure to pray. We must remember that unbelievers can get results by advertising and effort. Enthusiasm and effort will sell mousetraps or get decisions in evangelistic efforts, but prayer is a spiritual phenomenon commanded by the Word. First Chronicles 16:11; Matthew 7:7; 26:41; Luke 18:1; John 16:24; Ephesians 6:18; 1 Thessalonians 5:17; 1 Timothy 2:8 and James 5:13 and 16 are but a few instances from God's Word. The secret of effective prayer, therefore, is not only abiding in Christ and believing He will answer, but obeying and applying its necessity to our practice.

V. The Secret of Prayer Is Learning To Pray

Prayer is natural to men, but praying does not come naturally to men. All of us have probably heard the statement, "Prayer is to our spiritual life what breathing is to physical life." Also, "Prayer is the Christian's vital breath, the Christian's native air." Both statements are true, but this does not mean that all Christians pray or that those who do pray do so effectively. It is true that prayer, like breathing, is instinctive; but clearly there is a difference between the effectiveness of the prayer of a believer and that of an unbeliever. Also, there is a difference between the prayer of a young Christian and the prayer of a saint who has been practicing praying for years. In other words, the secret of prayer is learning to pray.

The disciples' petition in Luke 11:1, "Lord, teach us to pray," indicated that they had found something in the way Jesus prayed and the success He enjoyed in prayer. It implied that the method He used had in it technicalities in theory and practice that they wished to learn. If the disciples recognized the need to learn to pray, it is certainly true that we need to learn. If two people can read music and perform the same selection, yet demonstrate differing degrees of proficiency, it is apparent that practice is a significant factor.

Lindsell has a reference to a quotation from the great William James on the formation of good habits, assuming that we are persuaded to create good habits of prayer. James laid down these principles: Four rules might be summarized as follows: (1) The habit should be started with full self-commitment and with a "burning of bridges"; (2) the new action—in our case, prayer—should be repeated frequently, and if possible without lapse, especially in the early stages; (3) the impulse to obey it should be honored without delay, even if the impulse occurs "out of hours"; (4) the habit should be practiced beyond routine regularity and at some cost.

Need we say more? If you want to learn to pray, determine to do so and practice doing it. Reading books on prayer will not teach you to pray; engaging in prayer will! Practice makes perfect.

We intend to spend more time with techniques and mechanics in later lessons; so for now may we suggest that the Christian who desires to learn to pray set himself a time and place for regular prayer?

Establish certain habits and follow them. For example, read a portion of God's Word in order to put your mind in a proper attitude toward God and prayer. Often one verse will prove to be a challenge or a blessing. Kneel, stand or use any other posture which will promote freedom and comfort. Pray silently or aloud. The latter—even when one is alone—is to be preferred. Pray for people, places, things—anything. It may be helpful to list things about which to pray so you will not forget them. But above all—pray.

A brief résumé begins with the secret of prayer proving to be a combination of "abiding"—accepting Christ as one's personal Savior and resting in Him.

Then one must believe and claim the promises and statements of God's Word regarding prayer. He must obey the commands of the Lord and His Word with reference to prayer rather than just reading about them. Then practice until proficiency is obtained.

Prepare To Discuss Intelligently

1. Distinguish between *aulizomai* and *agrauleo*.
2. Complete the phrase: "The Church is looking for better methods; God is looking ———————."
3. List the four rules set forth by William James for establishing a habit.

Sources of Quotations

Bounds, E. M. *Power Through Prayer*. Grand Rapids: Zondervan Publishing House, 1972. Used by permission.

Lindsell, Harold. *When You Pray*. Wheaton, IL: Tyndale House Publishers, Inc., 1969, pp. 5, 13, 19, 21, 26, 60. Used by permission.

Murray, Andrew. *With Christ in the School of Prayer*. Grand Rapids: Zondervan Publishing House, p. 185. Used by permission.

CHAPTER 4

The Laws of Prayer

BIBLE PORTION TO READ: Luke 11:1-13

WE KNOW THAT GOD is the Creator of all
things "visible and invisible," those that are
tangible to the senses and those that are intangible and
cannot be comprehended by the senses; that is, in-
capable of being felt by touch. Colossians 1:16 and 17
make abundantly clear the fact that God in Christ
created, sustains and maintains all things, including
prayer. Just as it is necessary for us to learn the laws
of the physical universe and adjust to them whether or
not we understand them, so we must appropriate the
laws of the spiritual universe lest we suffer loss and
damage.

Spiritual laws are made known by revelation which
is contained in the Word of God. Ignorance of, neglect
of or rejection of either set of laws will neither inval-
idate or alter them.

From childhood we learn to respect gravitation, and
we use it to our advantage. We adjust our life-styles to
the sun and the seasons, and we benefit thereby; but by
some strange and irregular distortion of our mental
processes, we often live as though we can ignore or
violate spiritual laws with impunity.

How do we conclude that if a man does not know

26

God and has not heard the gospel (1 Cor. 15:1-4), he will nevertheless escape the wages of sin—physical and spiritual death?

Or suppose a man endeavors to live a good life, contributes to philanthropic causes and attends religious services—any kind, anytime, anywhere—will he then be saved? No! There are spiritual laws that apply—John 1:12; 5:24; 14:6; Romans 10:9 and 10 and Acts 16:31.

There are also spiritual laws, revealed only in God's Word, which cover such matters as giving. See Malachi 3:10 and 2 Corinthians 9. There are also laws covering matters of living—1 Corinthians 10:31; Colossians 3: 15-17—and prayer. It is this latter matter which is our concern and which is outlined for us in Luke 11. Here we will endeavor to learn the laws of prayer as Jesus presented them in the text of the prayer He taught His disciples in response to their petition, "Lord, teach us to pray."

Could I urge you to paraphrase this petition, "Lord, teach me to pray"?

I. First Law of Prayer—Addressed to God in Jesus' Name (Luke 11:2)

"Our Father which art in heaven, Hallowed be thy name." Also note the promise in John 14:13: "And whatsoever ye shall ask in my name, that will I do, that the Father may be glorified in the Son." We move from the glorious revelation of God revealed in His names given us in the Old Testament to the intimacy of the wonderful name of the Son, our Lord Jesus Christ. See the note in the old Scofield Reference Bible on Elohim, Genesis 1:1, and Jehovah, Genesis 2:4. Also check the Scofield subject-index under "Christ, the anointed" and the names following. Continue with John 15:16 and 16:24 and 26.

It is crystal clear that our access to God is in and through the name of Jesus Christ. It would seem to be patent that praying to or in the name of Buddha or

Mohammed or even through Peter, John or Mary would be ineffective, useless and probably even be an insult to the name of our wonderful Savior and Lord. This name, whether of God the Father or of Jesus Christ, is "hallowed"—holy and worthy of reverence. Yet the Lord Jesus Christ teaches us to use that name when we pray. I remind you that this law not only forbids and makes useless every other name, but it becomes exclusively the name which makes prayer valid.

What is in a name? We hear the phrase often. Andrew Murray (*With Christ in the School of Prayer*—Lesson 24) wrote: "When I mention or hear a name it calls up before me the whole man. . . .The name of a king includes his honour, his power, his kingdom. . . . And the Name of Christ is the expression of all He has done and all He is and lives to do as our Mediator." To come to God the Almighty in Jesus' name is to come with all the power and authority of His Son; it is with the assurance that the free use of that name provides unlimited resources.

Andrew Murray continued by indicating several aspects of and significance of the use of that name.

1. It may signify a legal union. I may call upon, ask for and use anything Jesus has because I have a legal right to sign His name on the purchase order when I pray. The verses cited above promise that the Father will honor any such request endorsed by the name of Jesus Christ.

2. It may signify a life union. I am a son of God; I bear the name of Christ, and my eyes have not seen nor my ears heard nor my heart imagined what my Heavenly Father has in store for His sons and daughters. Not only do I know the Son; I am a son (John 1: 12)!

3. It may signify a union of love. When a poverty-stricken, Hell-deserving sinner believes John 3:16 and responds with faith to the offer of Ephesians 2:8 and 9, he is saved, cleansed, made a new creature and—like

28

a bride—has a new name born of a love union with Christ. From now on the Lord Jesus Christ is obligated to His promise in Philippians 4:19.

As a born-again one I am legally united in life and in love to Jesus Christ and may freely use His name in prayer (Acts 4:12). Neither is there any other name acceptable in Heaven whereby we may draw on the vaults of grace and mercy (Heb. 4:16).

II. Second Law of Prayer—in the Will of God (Luke 11:2)

"Thy kingdom come. Thy will be done, as in heaven, so in earth." We have before remarked that "nothing lies outside the power and reach of prayer except that which lies outside the will of God."

Realizing that we are as children and therefore often do not know how to pray as we ought, it is necessary that we either know God's will as we pray or accept the response to our prayer as indicating His will. Who has not pleaded with God in utter sincerity and complete faith that God would provide what we were confident was "a need" or spare the life of a loved one, only to have the request denied? Perhaps it was a desire for a ten-speed bicycle, a lovely gown or an automobile, now clearly seen to have been a childish desire. However, not so easy was the continued illness or death of a loved one; but the grace that God supplied

29

has not only proved sufficient; but it has demonstrated the power, the love and goodness of God to many. Hence now we are able to pray, "Thy will be done," and accept the amendments to our praying that God finds necessary.

Surely the most lucid instance of prayer in the will of God is found in our Lord's prayer in the Garden of Gethsemane (Matt. 26:36-46). Three times Jesus prayed, "Let this cup pass from me: nevertheless not as I will, but as thou wilt." Without becoming involved in the technicalities of exegesis or theology, it is apparent to any thinking Christian that Jesus was not begging the Father that He might escape the cross; neither was He desperately seeking some other way to save sinners. His plea that the will of God be done in nowise infers that He did not know God's will or that He had misgivings about it. From the beginning He had known that Calvary was the plan; but as a Man, the agony of the impending ordeal had begun to force blood from His pores (Luke 22:44).

Knowing the power of Satan, Christ feared lest Satan might kill Him or He might collapse before He could reach the cross. It was then that Hebrews 5:7 became His experience and Matthew 26:39 His prayer.

The writer of Hebrews recorded: "Who in the days of his flesh," including Gethsemane, and very especially in Gethsemane, "when he had offered up prayers and supplications with strong crying and tears unto him that was able to save him from death, and was heard in that he feared." He was praying in the will of God to complete the plan for our redemption. Lord, teach us to pray!

Read again 1 John 5:13-15; ponder John 14:13 and 14. If you want God to answer your prayer, you must pray according to His will—not against it or without it. If you pray for things that will honor Him and please Him, it is certain that He will hear and answer. Remember, too, that God loves you and He loves to answer prayer. He is not trying to make it difficult to pray; neither is He trying to keep us seeking and never sure we have found His will. God loves us so much that He "spared not his own Son, but delivered him up for us all, how shall he not with him also freely give us all things?" (Rom. 8:32). See also Romans 5:10. He wants to give us all things richly to enjoy. Praying in His will is the way to get them.

III. Third Law of Prayer—Specific Requests (Luke 11:3, 4)

Consider Matthew 7:7 where we are instructed to "Ask . . . seek . . . knock." This is a verse that is familiar to all of us. The quesion is often asked; and even when it is not asked, we act as though we have serious question about the need to be specific when we pray. Too frequently we pray, "God bless this or that"; and evidently we take refuge in the fact that an all-knowing God, Who knows our thoughts and even the intents of our hearts, will figure out what it is we mean by "bless" and what we want for whom. We even pray for cleansing and generalize by assuming that when we "confess our sins," God knows which ones we mean; or He will automatically take care of all of them. Jesus is saying, "Ask for what you need; seek what you desire; knock when you want in," and conversely, "Do not expect results if you are not specific."

Read the reminders in James 4:2 and Isaiah 45:11.

Perhaps we are a bit uneasy to put out a fleece as did Gideon in Judges 6:36-39 lest we tempt God or err in ignorance, but God honored that specific prayer. In Genesis 24:12-14 we have the prayer of Abraham's servant when he sought a bride for Isaac. He certainly was most specific, and the Lord honored him for it.

We need to be reminded that if we are not definite in our asking, we will wander and grow careless and soon forget to pray. Also, we must remember that "we are not heard for our much speaking." As a matter of fact, much prayer may be "vain repetition" and virtually aimless. We need to be careful lest our children are allowed to recite bedtime and mealtime prayers as a matter of habit rather than intelligence or faith.

In his treatise on *Prayer, Asking and Receiving*, Dr. John R. Rice gives four good rules for becoming definite in prayer (Part III, chapter XI). These are as follows:

1. "Set out to weed out any objects of prayer about which you are not definite." Occasionally the intimate nature of a matter may warrant an "unspoken request"; but even your dearest friend cannot pray with you when he doesn't know what request to make.

2. "Next, set out to search the Scriptures and find in them the will of God." Wouldn't it be a help to remind God that 2 Peter 3:9 promises that God is "not willing that any should perish" when we pray for the unsaved by name? Doesn't Jeremiah 33:3 give us assurance and boldness in prayer? Also keep in mind the promises of Psalm 91:15; Isaiah 58:9; 65:24; John 15:7; 1 John 3:22 and 5:13-15.

3. Wait on God. "Let the Holy Spirit talk to you." Waiting for anyone or anything has become a lost art. We grow very impatient if we are kept waiting, especially when we have an appointment! Somehow we conclude that since "he ever liveth to make intercession for us," there is no need to waste time. The result of this is that we "say our prayers"; but there is little Holy Spirit direction possible. The Holy Spirit is supposed to "guide us into all truth," especially in prayer (John 16:13). He is ever interceding for us (Rom. 8:26).

4. Make a prayer list. This is suggested in spite of the danger of vain repetition. If the list is pointed and kept current by crossing out petitions that have been answered or by a note indicating when and where and how a prayer was answered, it can be a living thing and a real help to definite praying.

IV. Fourth Law of Prayer—Prayer with Desire and Intensity (Luke 11:5-10)

When Jesus finished the recitation of the so-called

"Lord's Prayer," He did not say, "Amen." Instead, He continued with the parable of the importunate friend. This seems to be a strange parable since the friend seemed to be very reluctant to help.

It is not difficult to imagine that God is our Friend and desires to help us. We readily admit that He has been much more faithful as a Friend than we have been. However, since He is our Friend, He promises not to ignore our need. But we must recognize our need and be specific in our praying; then the Lord will meet the need (Luke 11:8).

Perhaps a reference to Hannah as presented in 1 Samuel 1 would point out the importance of earnest, importunate prayer. Likewise would the example of Abraham and his intercession for Lot in Genesis 18:23-33 and the prayer of blind Bartimaeus as recorded in Mark 10:46-52 further point up this importance.

The Scriptures do not make clear why God requires evidence of sincerity and intensity in prayer; but it is He—not man—Who makes the laws. Most parents employ a very similar strategy when their children make requests. It is not unusual or improper; neither is it a sign of neglect or niggardliness that parents frequently ignore a child's request—which request is never repeated—and wait for the child to identify his need with desire. All children, including the children of God, have the "gimmees." Hence we wait until the request is narrowed down to a cookie or a sandwich. Perhaps God's insistence upon intensity is of like origin.

V. Fifth Law of Prayer—Results Are Guaranteed (Luke 11:11-13)

In this brief paragraph which follows immediately —and still on the same subject, prayer—Jesus picked up the likeness of God to an earthly parent and enlarged on the thought. First He assured us that God is as wise, loving and capable as any parent. Hence He will not give us bad things but rather will give us good things. It is better to go without than to give what will hurt. We must believe this! Not only must we believe that God is able and that He hears our prayers, but we also must believe that God answers our prayers in keeping with His wisdom and holiness.

It is the desire of every parent that his children grow up to know and understand his parent and to enter into the will and plans of the parent on a mature adult level. We are set upon a course which will cause us to grow up into Christ in all things—unto the stature of the fullness of Christ (Eph. 4:13, 15). How better could our loving Father do this than by giving the Holy Spirit to us to guide, direct and instruct?

Let us learn well the laws of prayer.

1. All prayer is validated by our relationship to God through Jesus Christ.

2. Our prayers are limited only by the will of God.

3. Prayer is activated by boldness and clarity before the Throne of Grace.

4. Our prayers are effectuated by earnestness of heart and purpose.

5. Our prayers are consummated in the purposes and promises of God.

Prepare To Discuss Intelligently

1. List the five laws of prayer.

2. List the three uses of a name which we employ when we pray.

3. List Dr. John R. Rice's rules for definite prayer.

Sources of Quotations

Lindsell, Harold. "The Laws Governing Prayer," *When You Pray*. Wheaton, IL: Tyndale House Publishers, Inc., 1969, pp. 60, 62. Used by permission.

Murray, Andrew. *With Christ in the School of Prayer*. Grand Rapids: Zondervan Publishing House, pp. 211-214. Used by permission.

CHAPTER 5

Reasons for Prayer

BIBLE PORTION TO READ: Philippians 3:1-21

THERE IS NO QUESTION that prayer is an integral element in religion, heathen as well as Christian. Every religion prays whether the one doing the praying is holding a broken shard as a talisman, whirling prayer wheels with prayers inside written on bits of paper or wafted on clouds of smoke from burning sacrifices or piles of incense. People pray when they are lying prostrate upon the ground headed toward Mecca, while plodding as flagellants with bloody backs, crawling on lacerated knees or kneeling with hands upstretched toward Heaven. But why do they do all these strange things when there is no merit in them?

Christians who believe in and practice prayer probably would rate far down the line if the time they spend in prayer, the fervency or frequency of that prayer were to be the standards. While all would agree that Christians *should* pray, many fail to do so. They seem to be saying, "Let me alone; I'm too busy having fun or making money or satisfying my own desires to take time to pray."

Why do you suppose that the hottest and most popular TV shows are on Sunday night or Wednesday night? The result of this is that while Muslims faithfully prostrate themselves three times a day and devotees of several Oriental religions drone monosyllabic chants hours on end, Christians say a hasty prayer at mealtime (but not always in public eating places), spend a minute or so in prayer upon arising in the morning and at bedtime and complain if the pastor's "long prayer" takes three minutes.

Why is this the case? Do we really believe in prayer? Have we ever analyzed the need, the reason or the cause for prayer? Why do we pray?

I. Because It Is a Sin Not To Pray

"Prayerlessness is sin." Do we believe it? "Prayer is the Christian's vital breath, the Christian's native air." Christians generally—and the local churches especially—are literally dying for lack of breath! Would it help if we actually believed that it is necessary to pray and it is sinful not to pray?

If there is any validity to the above statements, it means that we must pray. Not to do so is to commit spiritual suicide. Prayer—like breathing—should be involuntary. Couldn't it be true that 1 Thessalonians 5:17, "Pray without ceasing," has an application here? When we exert ourselves, our breathing is quickened and deepened. When we exert ourselves spiritually, praying becomes more active, quickened and deepened. In our spiritual lives every action must be fortified and strengthened by a greater voluntary effort in prayer.

Read 1 Samuel 12:23 and James 4:17. Could this mean that Jesus' remark in Luke 18:1, when coupled with the statement in James, literally makes it a sin for a Christian to neglect to pray? Could the "good works" of Ephesians 2:10 include prayer? Are we concerned about our sinful neglect of prayer?

Whether we are convinced that prayerlessness is indeed a sin of omission or not (James 4:17), it would seem certain that to contradict our Lord's statement in Luke 18:1 would be sin. Whether or not we agree that prayerlessness is fatal to spiritual life, it is certainly true that it is bound to produce spiritual anemia, spiritual mononucleosis or some other devitalizing ailment.

To deplore the state of the church or of society will be of little consequence if we do nothing about it. The enormity of the task may discourage us, but the size of the need should drive us to our knees in prayer. Satan is not too greatly concerned if we simply increase our activity, step up the budget or even attract larger crowds as long as prayer remains the province of the few. The presence of crowds in various kinds of services and programs will be largely ineffective as long as the Lord's people are content to engage in any activity while at the same time neglecting prayer.

E. M. Bounds in his book, *A Treasury of Prayer* (p. 22), has commented, "More praying will not come as a matter of course. The campaign for the twentieth or thirtieth century will not help, but hinder our praying if we are not careful. Many campaigns generate a great deal of activity, large crowds, much money, even many decisions, but little prayer. Nothing but a specific effort from praying leadership will avail. Praying apostles beget praying saints; a praying pulpit will beget praying pews. . . . We are a generation of nonpraying saints . . . a beggarly gang who have neither the ardor, nor beauty, nor power of saints."

Let us not explain our prayerlessness by calling it busyness, indolence or lethargy. Let's just call it sin, confess it, repent (turn about) and begin to pray.

II. Because God Commands Us To Pray and Jesus Christ Gives Us an Example To Follow

Norman B. Harrison *(His in a Life of Prayer)* wrote: "God is a great economist. As such He must anticipate every possible requirement for the continued existence, comfort and well-being of His creatures upon earth.

"But," he continued, "God is infinitely more than an economist. He is 'Our Father.'" As our Father, He requests us to "come boldly unto the throne of grace" (Heb. 4:16). We are also to ask, seek and knock (Matt. 7:7-11).

Jesus, God's Son, knew and obeyed God's will in the matter of prayer. Read Mark 1:35 and Luke 6:12. And for further insight into our Lord's prayer life, meditate on Luke 9:18 and 22:41.

In 1 Peter 2:21 Peter was talking about suffering rather than prayer, but I am bold to suggest it as applying to prayer: "Christ . . . leaving us an example, that ye should follow in his steps." Think, too, of all that is involved in the words of Hebrews 5:7 as you read it prayerfully.

"Men who belong to God are obliged to pray," wrote E. M. Bounds in his *Treasury of Prayer,* page 34. "They are not obliged to grow rich, nor to make money . . . to have large success in business. Men are neither better nor worse with these things or without them. . . . God is vitally concerned that men should pray. Men are bettered by praying. . . . God's greatest glory and man's highest good are secured by prayer."

Look up and read the following: 1 Chronicles 16:11; Matthew 26:41; John 16:24; James 5:13; Deuteronomy 4:29; Psalm 105:4; Isaiah 55:6; Hosea 10:12; Amos 5:4; Zephaniah 2:3 and Matthew 6:33.

III. Because It Is Our Job As Believer-Priests

Probably every believer has read 1 Peter 2:5 and 9: "Ye also, as lively stones, are built up a spiritual house, an holy priesthood, to offer up spiritual sacrifices, acceptable to God by Jesus Christ. . . . But ye are a chosen generation, a royal priesthood, an holy nation, a peculiar people; that ye should shew forth the praise of him who hath called you out of darkness into his marvellous light."

When the Lord Jesus Christ ascended on high, He took up the office of High Priest; and we became believer-priests. God has gifted some men for special service as "apostles . . . prophets . . . evangelists . . . pastors and teachers [or pastor-teachers]" (Eph. 4:11); but He has commissioned all believers as priests as is recorded in the First Epistle of Peter. The so-called laymen—no less than the pastor—and the pastor—no more than the laymen—have the official responsibility to offer up spiritual sacrifices. There may be several ways this can be done, but I am sure that one way is in this ministry of prayer!

In the same verse (John 15:16) where we are called of God to bring forth fruit that remains, the only actual responsibility Christ mentions is, "Whatsoever ye shall ask the Father in my name, he may give it you." These words are followed immediately by, "These things I command you, that ye love one another." Prayer for and love to the brethren would seem to be the first, if not the primary, function of these believer-priest-servants.

Can you imagine what might happen to such a priest who neglected, perverted or prostituted his office? Look up what happened to Nadab and Abihu as recorded in Leviticus 10:1-7. Also note what happened to the sons of Eli—Hophni and Phineas (1 Sam. 2:12-17; 4:11) and to the sons of Samuel—Joel and Abiah (1 Sam. 8:1-6). Could it not be that the impotence of the church in our day is due in some measure to the caliber of those who are believer-priests within it?

IV. Because We Owe It to Our Family

A. One of the first things we recognize when we are

saved is that we have become a part of the family of God: "But as many as received him, to them gave he power to become the sons of God, even to them that believe on his name" (John 1:12). The same fact is made clear in Ephesians 2:19: "Now therefore ye are no more strangers and foreigners, but fellowcitizens with the saints, and of the household of God." See, too, Romans 8:15 where we read: "Ye have received the Spirit of adoption, whereby we cry, Abba, Father." And 2 Corinthians 6:11-18 reminds us that we ought to act like the children of God, especially in our separation from the old life. The Lord said, "And [I] will be a Father unto you, and ye shall be my sons and daughters, saith the Lord Almighty."

Galatians 3:26 bears out the same truth: "For ye are all the children of God by faith in Christ Jesus." And we are reminded in Romans 8:16: "The Spirit itself beareth witness with our spirit, that we are the children of God."

First John 3:10 gives the strong reminder, "In this the children of God are manifest . . . whosoever doeth not righteousness is not of God, neither he that loveth not his brother." And 1 John 5:2 states, "By this we know that we love the children of God, when we love God and keep his commandments."

This love within the family of God—which is often stronger than our love for blood relatives—is at first a surprise but always a thrill. We are concerned for one another and are admonished to "bear . . . one another's burdens" (Gal. 6:2). We very soon recognize the truth that in the body of Christ when one member suffers or rejoices, the other members share with that suffering or rejoicing (1 Cor. 12:26, 27). We begin at once to pray one for another, and this is as it should be. Would it not be inconsistent if it were otherwise? See 1 John 2:6 and 4:7-12 ("Beloved, let us love one another"). These references are speaking of the family.

B. Many texts enjoin family prayer and evidence the effectiveness of it. "Again I say unto you, That if two of you shall agree on earth as touching any thing that they shall ask, it shall be done for them of my Father which is in heaven" (Matt. 18:19).

Following the discourse on the Christian's armor in Ephesians 6:11-17, Paul pleaded that we would pray, supplicate, watch and persevere "for all saints; and for me" (vv. 18, 19). In every Epistle Paul wrote he reminded those to whom he was writing that he was praying for them often, mentioning by name the people and the needs and urging a sharing in prayer. (See Ephesians 1:15-23 and Colossians 1:9ff. as examples.)

The union of believers in the Body of Christ and our union as the children of God upon earth presents a claim upon us to pray for one another, being "mindful of the welfare one of another" as we read in our church covenants.

V. Because We Owe It to the Unsaved

The soul-winning ministry of prayer is recognized by most Christians, but it has yet to come home with conviction. We live in the midst of a world that is plunging toward judgment and into Hell with frightening rapidity. Hundreds whose names we know are unsaved, doomed and damned; yet we stand by as though there is nothing we can do about it. We weakly explain that they "want to do their own thing"; therefore, we let them. We are shocked by the increase of cults, even that of Satanism. We are distressed by the numbers of people who are going into Oriental, philosophical religions. We are critical of methods being employed to reach the masses with something—anything that is called "the gospel"; but at the same time we are strangely dry eyed and prayerless, to say nothing of being indolent!

We know that the Scriptures say, "For God so loved the world, that he gave his only begotten Son, that whosoever believeth in him should not perish, but have everlasting life" (John 3:16). We know that God is "not willing that any should perish, but that all should come

41

to repentance" (2 Pet. 3:9). We understand the intentions of God "who will have all men to be saved" (1 Tim. 2:4). We know about the Great Commission (Matt. 28:19, 20). We know about the ministry of the Holy Spirit to "reprove the world of sin . . . because they believe not on me" (John 16:8, 9). We are convinced that "without faith it is impossible to please him [God]" (Heb. 11:6) and that "faith cometh by hearing, and hearing by the word of God" (Rom. 10:17). But do we pray?

Norman B. Harrison in *His in a Life of Prayer* has noted, "A study of the Gospels yields this interesting and instructive fact regarding faith [prayer] for others: as far as the record states the circumstances, three times as many were healed and helped through the intercession of others as obtained this blessing through their own asking." For example, read Mark 2:1-12. Notice verse 5 in this portion: "When Jesus saw their faith [the four], he said unto the sick of the palsy, Son, thy sins be forgiven thee." A man had his sins forgiven and his body healed because his friends were concerned enough to pray and bring him into touch with Jesus!

Harrison has also cited the woman of Canaan (Matt. 15:21-28) whose daughter was "vexed with a devil." The disciples wanted to send her away because she was not a Jew, but her persistence brought from Jesus the words, "O woman, great is *thy* faith: be it *unto thee* even as thou wilt. And *her daughter* was made whole from that very hour."

Do you suppose we could help the present generation of young people, some of them our own sons and daughters, some of them grievously vexed with demons, dope and depravity, if we would pray? Do you suppose that if parents agreed together in Jesus' name (Matt. 18:19), they could assure the salvation of their children or their protection from and deliverance from "the wiles of the devil" (Eph. 6:11)? We recognize that prayer has played a major role in every revival of consequence;

but do we realize that if any two of us really got down to business in prayer, we could be prime movers in soul-winning!

Perhaps it ought not be said, but one must be shocked at the paucity of reference to prayer as an adjunct in soul-winning. We find no chapter in any book we have examined on the place of prayer in winning souls to Christ. There are numerous references to the subject, but seldom is there as much space given to it as is accorded here. Do we really believe in praying for souls? Are we really concerned about lost souls?

Again, we quote E. M. Bounds: "Prayer is not merely a question of duty, but of salvation. Are men saved who are not men of prayer? Can it be possible to be in affinity with Jesus Christ and not be prayerful? Can brotherly love be in the heart who is unschooled in prayer?" To this, the Word of God adds: "Ask of me, and I shall give thee the heathen [unsaved] for thine inheritance" (Ps. 2:8). True, Psalm 2 is a Messianic Psalm; but could it possibly apply to us who as believer-priests are bidden to go into all the world seeking the lost, heathen, unsaved? Do we dare pray for souls? Do we dare *not* pray for souls?

Prepare To Discuss Intelligently

1. Quote a three-word command given as a reason for prayer.

2. Write down three sets of Old Testament "P.K.s" (preachers' kids) who failed God because their parents neglected their duties. How does this apply to us as believer-priests?

3. Discuss Matthew 18:19 in connection with soul-winning.

4. How does 1 Peter 2:5-9 make us responsible to pray?

CHAPTER 6

Hindrances to Prayer

BIBLE PORTION TO READ: Psalm 37:1-11

THERE IS ALMOST NO END to the things which could be listed under the general heading of hindrances to prayer. Everyone has been distracted by the telephone, the TV or a loud radio. We have all had the distressing experience of our minds' wandering while we prayed, of woolgathering or, worse yet, dropping off to sleep. Is there anyone who has ever tried to pray and simply could not concentrate; who was so emotionally upset as to be unable to pray or was so burdened that he found it impossible to put into words an intelligible prayer?

These things would seem to be simple enough that we could handle them if we tried. Therefore, we will put forth our efforts here in considering some hindrances which, being more subtle or stronger or longer lasting, are so deeply grained into our very nature and personal temperament as to appear unbreakable.

While all of us would probably agree that we should pray and pray more, each one is concerned about failure. Each person blames his failure on many things, but seldom have we really taken time to sit down to identify realistically and honestly why we fail or what we need to do about this failure. Let us attempt to do so in this chapter.

I. Laziness

Certainly the most common hindrance—if not the most effective—is just plain laziness. This is true in other areas as well. We complain about not having time to pray or read or study God's Word or a score of other things that we really ought to do. Perhaps we should do as a dean at college requires of students whose grades are failing: Take an objective look at things.

Take a sheet of paper and make several columns the length of the paper, each column an inch or so wide. Line the paper crosswise with spaces about a half inch wide so that you end up with sets of two columns; one 1″ x ½″ and the other, about 1½″ wide. In the left column write a sequence of time in fifteen-minute segments; e.g.: 8:00—8:15, 8:15—8:30, etc. Continue down the page and in succeeding columns until your normal bedtime. Now endeavor to note in the next column to the right what you did each fifteen minutes all day. It will take several days to get into the habit of jotting things down at least every hour or so. In about that many days, you will become aware of the fact that you are really hard pressed to account for many minutes —maybe hours—each day.

Next, fill in several spaces such as lunch time, coffee break or things you do pretty much on schedule each day. Now insert—at some convenient point— fifteen minutes for Bible reading and prayer. See if you can manage one such period in the morning and one in the evening. By now you will be forced to admit that the time is available, and you will wonder why it has not been evident before. It may also appear that indolence, lack of effort and carelessness are more to blame for our lack of prayer than is lack of time.

A. Not all laziness is the same. Not all people are indolent about everything. If they are, they should see a doctor. Usually we are interested and active in some areas while being ineffective in others. Boys often have plenty of get up and go about anything pertaining

"Now unto him that is able to do exceeding abundantly above all that we ask or think, according to the power that worketh in us, unto him be glory in the church by Christ Jesus throughout all ages, world without end. Amen" (Eph. 3:20, 21).

"For the eyes of the Lord are over the righteous, and his ears are open unto their prayers: but the face of the Lord is against them that do evil" (1 Pet. 3:12).

to athletics, but they have great difficulty with reading or homework. Girls may find planning a party or making a dress interesting, but such is not the case with practicing the piano or helping with housework. We need to take ourselves in hand and discipline ourselves to do what we ought to do regardless of how we feel in the matter. To do this will reduce the problem, eliminate the hindrance and create character.

We need to do as the Lord Jesus did in Gethsemane. In Luke 22:44 we read, "He prayed more earnestly." Literally, "He became in agony as He prayed."

James wrote of the prophet Elijah: "Elias . . . prayed earnestly [fervently]."

Paul commended Epaphras for "always labouring fervently [literally, agonizing] for you in prayers" (Col. 4:12).

We simply and sincerely need to *make ourselves* spend time in prayer. Call it "Operation Bootstrap" if you wish. Never was it more true that "God helps them who help themselves" than is the case in prayer.

B. Another form of this problem might be called *ergophobia*—fear of work. Not only do we soon discover that it takes time to pray, but we find that prayer is hard work. Simple "Now I lay me down to sleep" prayers may not be difficult to repeat; but when we begin to share the burdens of others or supplicate God with real concern, it becomes work. Sometimes it is not so much that prayer has been neglected as it is that it has been found to be hard work and thus discontinued.

Perhaps the parable in Luke 18:1-8 is a case in point, especially the thought in verses 7 and 8: "And shall not God avenge his own elect, which cry day and night unto him, though he bear long with them? I tell you that he will avenge [vindicate, respond in keeping with His law] them speedily." Again it is prayer *and* work which get results. It is not prayer instead of work or lack of prayer because it is work!

C. A third form of this hindrance might be called dereliction of duty. In the Garden of Gethsemane our Lord told Peter, "Watch and pray, lest ye enter into temptation. The Spirit truly is willing, but the flesh is weak" (Mark 14:38). We know what Jesus meant by observing what happened. Peter and the other disciples fell asleep. When that happens to a sentry on duty, he is court-martialed. The sentry will have a hard time explaining why he fell asleep, and the most extenuating circumstances will be needed to secure leniency.

The word "watch" in Jesus' statement is probably the key. Jesus knew these men were tired; He knew it was late at night; He was not scolding them. However, they were His disciples, and He was asking them to pray with Him. He asked them to be alert, to be vigilant, literally to "stay awake." Instead, they went to sleep! Special effort was expected and requested; but they—and we—are just too tired or lazy or both. God forgive us!

II. Circumstances

There are circumstances which hinder, and their number is legion.

A. *Domestic Conditions.* First Peter 3:7 bluntly implies that failure to dwell together intelligently will hinder the prayers of husbands and wives. It will upset them on occasion so that they do not care to pray; and it will prevent them from most effective prayer because they are not united in prayer. See Matthew 18:19: "Again I say unto you, That if two of you shall agree on earth as touching any thing." Any two! Which two should be more able to agree? By the same token, these two frequently—more often than most—are liable to disagree.

Doctors declare that many disorders, ulcers and nervous conditions result from domestic disharmony. Auto insurance people place high on the list of causes of accidents this same disharmony between husbands and wives. Since prayer is a spiritual exercise—much more delicate and sensitive than these—it is easy to see that lack of understanding, lack of spiritual harmony, to say nothing of discord, could and does hinder prayer.

How important it is that we be one in Christ, not unequally yoked. How significant is the attention necessary to the command thrice given in Ephesians 5:25, 28 and 33: "Husbands love your wives." How necessary is the attitude of the wife who is to "reverence—respect" her husband, "submit—fall in alongside according to rank" (Eph. 5:33, 22) and even "obey—take second place" (Titus 2:5).

How needful it is that these two meet to share their burdens in prayer with singleness of heart and with the wisdom God promises to them that ask (James 1:5).

The husband's tendency to ignore and neglect his wife hinders a wife from joining heartily in prayer. The inclination of wives to make special efforts to look nice and be nice to everyone else, but to treat their husbands as though they were necessary evils, hinders prayer.

B. *Ignorance.* In this case it means the ignorance resulting from careless thinking about God and the will of God as revealed in the Word of God. We read in Mark 9:23: "If thou canst believe, all things are possible to him that believeth"; and we assume that, because we

48

are believers, we can ask for and expect anything and everything. However, we also need to read Isaiah 55:8 and 9: "For my thoughts are not your thoughts, neither are your ways my ways, saith the LORD. For as the heavens are higher than the earth, so are my ways higher than your ways, and my thoughts than your thoughts."

Prayer is governed by spiritual laws which are covered elsewhere in this series. Ignorance of these laws—and of the person of God—hinders prayer. We may laugh at the child who questions, "Can God make a rock so big that He cannot lift it?" Yet with like naivete we may ask God for foolish things, unnecessary things, unscriptural things, forgetting that God—even though He is infinite and omnipotent—cannot do that which is inconsistent with His nature. The laws of the universe are not likely to be abridged or abrogated because we pray. Neither is God likely to take from us the consequences of our foolishness or sin even though we pray.

The Scriptures do not give detailed instruction on every subject, but a sensitive spirit—informed by the Scriptures and guided by the Holy Spirit—will not be hindered by ignorance.

C. *Rebellion and Self-Will.* These are hindrances to prayer. Such hindrances stem from the desire to have our own way, not from contrariness. Too often our prayer is like a child who says, "I want *what* I want *when* I want it," and who will not take "no" for an answer.

In 1 Samuel 8:7-22 Israel wanted a king. No explaining or reasoning would cause them to change their minds. The text does not indicate that they prayed, but it surely can be assumed that they did. They besought God—not for something bad, but for something they wanted "like all the nations"—and it hindered their praying and hindered God from answering, even though He did accede to their desires: "And ye shall cry out in that day because of your king which ye shall have chosen you; and the LORD will not hear you in that day. Nevertheless the people refused to obey the voice of Samuel; and they said, Nay; but we will have a king over us" (1 Sam. 8:18, 19).

This rebellion is often expressed in dissatisfaction with what God is doing. We want skies that are always blue, weather that is neither too hot nor too cold; and our unhappiness with the rain hinders our prayers. We should read the old hymn:

> "God hath not promised
> Skies always blue,
> Flower-strewn pathways
> All our lives through."

The heart that kicks against the circumstances, whatever they be, will find that his prayer is hindered. It is better to accept things as part of the "all things [that] work together for good" and as "every good and every perfect gift" (Rom. 8:28; James 1:17); and, having a peaceful heart, each believer should pray effectively.

III. Impatience Hinders Prayer

Harold Lindsell has remarked, "Patience is a virtue praised by many, possessed by few, and sought only occasionally." When we pray, we want God to answer our requests immediately. If He delays, we become impatient (1 Sam. 13). If God answers differently from what we asked or expected, we complain and become impatient with Him. David urged: "Rest in the LORD, and wait patiently for him" (Ps. 37:7). James also has reminded us, "Knowing this, that the trying of your faith worketh patience" (1:3).

Patience is repeatedly enjoined upon believers. In James 5:7 and 8 the subject under consideration is the Lord's return, and we are urged to be patient. Romans 5:3 and 4 remind us that "tribulation worketh patience; and patience, experience; and experience, hope." Then in Romans 8:25 it says that hope in turn

50

generates more patience. Romans 15:5 reads, "Now the God of patience and consolation grant you to be like-minded one toward another according to Christ Jesus." In other words, it would appear that God might very reasonably choose to answer our prayers in a manner that would build patience. Therefore, impatience would definitely be a hindrance.

God usually uses ordinary channels and natural phenomena in answering prayers, rather than using miracles; thus it may take longer. God is more likely to comfort you in the darkness than He is to hasten the dawn. Do not be impatient.

Along this line, notice Acts 12:5-19. Here we have an example of persistence rather than impatience, and it merits our emulation. Someone has said, "It is always too soon to quit"; and this is very especially true of prayer. God *wants* to answer our prayers. Notice the following:

Ephesians 3:20: "Now unto him that is able to do exceeding abundantly above all that we ask or think, according to the power that worketh in us."

I Corinthians 2:9: "But it is written, Eye hath not seen, nor ear heard, neither have entered into the heart of man, the things which God hath prepared for them that love him."

IV. Wrong Motives Hinder Prayer

This is a difficult area because we must judge our own motives, and we usually justify ourselves. However, Jesus recognized this propensity and cited a glaring example in Matthew 6:1-7.

A. In almsgiving there is the motive of receiving glory of men. Few can resist the temptation to let somebody know that they have made a substantial contribution. Jesus says, "Keep it a secret, even from your other hand; and God will reward you openly."

B. In prayer there is the motive of being seen of men. Jesus said literally, "Go into your closet and do your praying, and let the answers be your gratification." In

When You Pray, Harold Lindsell mentioned that the hypocrisy involves not only the desire to be considered saintly but also a subtle desire to manipulate God. When we have prayed publicly, we like to think that we have placed God under obligation to defend His honor by honoring our prayers. Such behavior is childish.

C. James 4:3 makes it clear that if we want selfish gratification, we may as well not ask: "Ye ask, and receive not, because ye ask amiss, that ye may consume it upon your lusts." This may not be carnal gratification such as "things," but even normal desires such as the salvation of a husband or wife "because it would make life so much easier."

The desire to hold office is a good thing (1 Tim. 3:1); but if such a desire is not guarded, it may contribute to pride and thus be harmful. In such a case, God would not be likely to answer. To sing a solo as contributing to the worship service may be prompted by self-interest. Many problems have been created in choirs by such desires, even though someone prayed about getting to sing the solo.

Wrong motives betray weakness in character which will produce dishonesty and jeopardize our moral fiber as well as our prayer life. Let's be honest with God and ourselves when we pray.

V. Other Wrong Motives

Space forbids continuing, but it will be well to continue your study by reading the following:

Matthew 5:23-25: "Therefore if thou bring thy gift to the altar, and there rememberest that thy brother hath ought against thee; leave there thy gift before the altar, and go thy way; first be reconciled to thy brother, and then come and offer thy gift. Agree with thine adversary quickly, whiles thou art in the way with him; lest at any time the adversary deliver thee to the judge, and the judge deliver thee to the officer, and thou be cast into prison."

Matthew 6:14 and 15: "For if ye forgive men their trespasses, your heavenly Father will also forgive you: but if ye forgive not men their trespasses, neither will your Father forgive your trespasses."

Ephesians 4:31, 32: "Let all bitterness, and wrath, and anger, and clamour, and evil speaking, be put away from you, with all malice: and be ye kind one to another, even as God for Christ's sake hath forgiven you."

Read Matthew 18:21-35 and Luke 19:1-10 in addition. Examine the effects of wrong motives upon prayer.

VI. Unconfessed Sin

Similarly, unconfessed sin will hinder prayer.

A. Covetousness, which is a common American trait, will blight prayer. Read the following Scriptures to see how this fact is confirmed: Malachi 3:8, 9; Colossians 3:5; Ephesians 5:5 and 1 Timothy 6:10. The cure for this sin is tithing (Mal. 3:10).

B. Iniquity, too, will hinder prayer as we see in Psalm 66:18 and Isaiah 59:1 and 2. The remedy for this is found in Psalm 139:23 and 24 and 1 John 1:9. God help us to get the hindrances out.

Prepare To Discuss Intelligently

1. Which hindrance to prayer do you consider to be most effective for you? What can you do about it?

2. How important is the matter of harmony between husband and wife and prayer at your house? Do you pray aloud together?

3. Have you ever found an occasion to resist a covetous spirit and had victory in prayer as a result?

4. Discuss James 4:1-4. Do you suppose weakness in prayer and carnality could be suggested in verse 4 as failure or neglect is suggested in verse 2?

Source of Quotations

Lindsell, Harold. *When You Pray.* Wheaton, IL: Tyndale House Publishers, Inc., 1969, pp. 114, 115, 120, 121, 128. Used by permission.

CHAPTER 7

Problems
(Part I)

BIBLE PORTION TO READ: 2 Corinthians 12:6-11

IN DR. JOHN R. RICE'S great work, *Prayer—Asking and Receiving,* chapter IV, he calls our attention to James 4:2 and Matthew 7:7. Then he says: "Many, many Scriptures show that prayer, in the Bible sense, is asking God definitely for something."

"Now there is another side to that truth," avers Dr. Rice. "If prayer is asking, then the answer to prayer must be receiving. It is the will of our loving heavenly Father that we should be able to come to Him day by day, ask what we want, and receive it."

However, Dr. Rice adds, "Preachers have a way, when faith grows dim and weak, of making alibis for the fruitlessness of their prayers. For example, preachers sometimes say, 'God answers prayer in three ways. He may say, 'Yes' or He may say, 'No,' or He may say, 'Wait awhile.' "

Such a statement is considered by Dr. Rice to make prayer "a mystical, indefinite matter, by which one may get what he wants, or he may not, as if there were no way to know what is the will of God. It leaves the impression that there is not much use praying, because God will do what pleases Him anyway without any meddling of ours, so why should we pray?"

The problem we discuss is created by a basic disagreement with the statement that God always answers prayer affirmatively, plus the need for an explanation for unanswered prayer. Dr. Harold Lindsell in his fine book *When You Pray*, chapter V, says: "Prayer has its problems. You may minimize them, avoid them, or pretend they do not exist, but they remain." Dr. Lindsell continues, "The finite human mind cannot fully fathom the divine mind and God has not given quick and easy answers to all the questions we ask." Isaiah 55:8 and 9 surely declare as much.

"The Christian mind tends to oversimplify the problems," asserts Dr. Lindsell, "because of a mind-set that often thinks. . .'black-white,' 'either-or,' 'yes-no.' This mind-set just doesn't see the large areas of gray that are neither black nor white. Just as it is impossible in some situations to assert dogmatically that one course of action or another is right or wrong, so there are no easy and dogmatic answers to the many and difficult problems connected with prayer."

"God answers our prayers one of three ways," firmly asserts Lindsell. "He may say 'yes,' He may say 'no' and He may say 'later.' When God says 'no,' the very act of denial creates problems for us," agrees Lindsell. However, he does not feel that it is correct to say that we have not truly prayed or that prayer was defective or that the prayer was not in accord with the will of God. "This forces us," he declares, "to focus our attention on some of the knotty and hard-to-resolve problems. . . . It is still valuable to face up to problems we cannot fully solve and for which we do not always have final answers. We may have to conclude that there is nothing that we can do except to throw ourselves on the mercy of God and wait patiently for the turn of events in the midst of the inscrutable mystery of His sovereignty."

"In some instances we can draw definite conclusions and devise specific solutions," Dr. Lindsell offers. We must do this "in order to gain perspective and develop a richer and fuller prayer life."

Let us examine these two positions more carefully:

I. God Always Answers Prayer Affirmatively

Based upon the statement, "And whatsoever we ask, we receive" (1 John 3:22), we conclude that God always says "yes" in answer to prayer.

There is no doubt that most of us too often have looked upon prayer as a convenience which, when used, produces remarkable results. However, all have experienced problems in prayer since we do not always receive answers to our prayers. Usually we accept the dictum often propounded, "God always answers prayer; but sometimes He says 'yes'; sometimes 'no' and sometimes 'wait awhile.'" Some feel that such an attitude is an insult to God's veracity and integrity and is a cruel trifling with the souls of men.

Dr. John R. Rice quotes Dr. Charles A. Blanchard in his book, *Getting Things from God,* as disagreeing with the idea that God sometimes does not answer, or instead says "no." "I think," wrote Dr. Blanchard, "it would tend to make infidels rather than Christians."

Dr. Blanchard went on to insist, "An answer to prayer is a granting of the thing which a child asks of his heavenly Father, according to the directions which his Father has clearly set down. . . . Saying 'no' to a request is not an answer to prayer in any real, substantial meaning of the expression. When God answers prayer He says 'yes'" asserts the good doctor. "To say that the answer may be 'yes' or 'no' and that the latter is as much an answer as the former, seems to me trifling with the sore hearts and the great needs of man."

Dr. Rice then picks up the theme and contends, "All of us know that the average Christian does not usually get exactly what he asks from God. On the contrary, the average Christian expects nothing of the kind. His prayers are indefinite; they do not pointedly and plainly ask for concrete, definite answers."

"Doubtless," continues Dr. Rice, "this is the reason that so many Christians condition nearly every request with the words, 'if it be Thy will.' "

We must agree that too often when we ask God for revival, conversion of sinners, bread, a fish or an egg and add "if it be Thy will," we are not expressing submission to God's will but to our unbelief. What God has promised, He will give and do; we dare not place a question mark behind the promises of God.

Several excellent suggestions made by Dr. Rice would seem to guarantee that our praying will be in the will of God and thus assure us of an affirmative response. Consider these examples:

A. Read Psalm 37:4. Would you expect God to answer the prayer of one who denied the truth of our Lord's virgin birth? Or the inspiration of the Scriptures? Or the efficacy of the precious blood? Would you expect God to meet your need because you are His child, but knowing that you are committing a particular sin? Read Psalm 66:18.

Should we expect God to consider our unspoken requests when He has given us the warning of James 4:2? Or again, would you expect God to answer a prayer for blessing on a business so that we will have the money to pay off a debt we incurred through poor judgment and in order to escape disclosure, embarrassment or prosecution? Read James 4:3. Then look up and read George Stebbins' hymn "Have Thine Own Way, Lord."

B. There must be a recognition of and surrender to

57

God's will or we may as well save our breath. But when we "delight ourselves in the Lord" and pray, we have the petitions we desire. This is the contention of both Dr. Rice and Dr. Blanchard. That we can know, and therefore pray, in God's will is possible because we have access to His Word wherein His will is revealed. Read again Psalm 1, especially the first three verses. Read Joshua 1:7-9 and note that in both instances the guarantees of God's blessing are based upon meditating day and night on the Word.

We cannot assume that a hurried reading of a few verses of Scripture, followed by a word or a season of prayer, will accomplish for us a "yes" answer to our prayers. Meditation surely implies time spent with the Word so that we know and understand the will of God so thoroughly that we can pray with assurance and with the assurance of answers.

C. Then, too, even with all our knowledge, we frequently "know not what we should pray for as we ought" (Rom. 8:26, 27). It is then that "the Spirit also helpeth our infirmities" and "maketh intercession . . . according to the will of God." The indwelling Holy Spirit will guide us and make our prayers pleasing to God so that He can answer affirmatively.

Praying with confidence that God will say "yes" is the only way to pray, affirms Dr. Rice; and he concludes that (1) a surrendered will on our part, (2) a knowledge of God's will as revealed in the Bible, and (3) submitting to the guidance of the Holy Spirit as we pray, is prayer. Less than this is a mere pious platitude or pharisaical much speaking. "If you do not get just what you pray for, then you should set out today to find out what is wrong with your prayers," according to the good doctor.

II. Sometimes God Says 'Yes,' 'No' or 'Wait'

As is usually the case, men of God do not contradict one another as much as they simply present things from differing vantage points. The "God always answers 'yes' " position sees prayer from the vantage point of simple, literal and Scriptural statements. But all of us, even the most literal fundamentalists, have problems about unanswered prayer. From the vantage point of our own personal experience, we have very real problems. In our personal prayer lives God sometimes says "no" or "wait."

Certainly we do not place experience above Scripture. Many of the errors of our day are based on experience rather than plain facts of Bible truth, and we would not contribute to these errors by including prayer along with miracles and tongues. However, we cannot avoid, deny or minimize the fact that God does not always say "yes" to this author's prayers. On several occasions over forty years in the gospel ministry this author has had to face the impossible situation of explaining to a grieving wife or mother or a widowed father why God said "no."

On the one hand prayer is as simple as breathing; but it is also as complex as the things about which we pray. Read Isaiah 55:8 and 9. Thus, when God's thoughts are clearly revealed, we can pray positively and assuredly; but when our thoughts and emotions become involved—and they almost always do—things can get mixed up no matter how fundamental or sincere we may be. It would appear that we can pray and, in so doing, exhaust our knowledge of God and the Word of God while still being so far short of God's thoughts in a particular matter as to make it necessary for God to say "no" or "wait until you grow a little older."

In *When We Pray*, page 78, Dr. Harold Lindsell suggests that Israel prayed to God for meat (Num. 11) which God gave them; but Psalm 106:15 indicates that the request had been contrary to the will of God and hence was not good for them. But God granted it! How do we explain that?

Hezekiah had a word from God in 2 Kings 20:1; but in answer to prayer, God gave Hezekiah fifteen more years of life. During those fifteen years Manasseh was born. He became king and dishonored God and disgraced his own parents. Also, Hezekiah committed political blunders that spoiled the image he had created, even including the miracle of added years. If such can be the case, we had better pray, "Thy will be done," lest our asking be amiss since our finite minds cannot know the mind of God.

Again, when Paul prayed for the removal of the thorn in his flesh, God did not say "no." However, He certainly did say "not now" and promised, "My grace is sufficient for thee" (2 Cor. 12:7-11).

Shadrach, Meshach and Abed-nego knew the will of God with regard to idols, but they did not know the mind of God with reference to the furnace (Dan. 3:17, 18). They were willing to take "no" for an answer and could not have known what God would do. Often we find ourselves in like positions. Shall we refuse to pray until we are sure God will say "yes," or should we pray "if it be Thy will"?

Hebrews 11:32-40 records faithful saints who wrought miracles but also those who were "tortured . . . had trial of cruel mockings and scourgings . . . received not the promise." In other words, God said "yes" to some but "no" to others. If we who are parents are wise enough not to give a 22-caliber pistol to a child, ought not God in His infinite wisdom be allowed to say "no" to our requests?

Even a "maybe" or "wait awhile" would seem to be entirely proper when one looks at prayer from the angle of man's knowledge and experience. In many things, the passing of time reveals what to us was not plain at an earlier time. We prayed earnestly, but now we know that denial or delay was the right answer. Ought we not to trust God, our all-wise Heavenly Father, to make the choices for us? Ought we not to be willing to pray, "if it be Thy will"? Is this cruel or faithless? I think not.

The author recalls earnest, fervent prayer regarding a 1936 Ford. It was a need in the Lord's work; but much pleading with God, the bank and a brother resulted in "no" for an answer. However, a year later the same brother made us a gift of a 1939 Chevy, which three years later was surrendered to a dealer to obtain a new 1946 Plymouth, a gift of the church. Who would refuse to praise God for a "no" which was in reality only "wait awhile"?

We know that God hears and answers prayer, but we shall be forever children while we dwell on the earth. Hence we will pray confidently; and much of the time we will be in God's will, taught by God's Word and directed by the Holy Spirit. Sometimes our best and most sincere prayers will need to be concluded with "Thy will be done." God will always answer "yes," "no" and occasionally "wait." In the latter case, we can expect something better later.

We do not feel that Dr. Rice or Dr. Blanchard are wrong. Neither do we believe that Dr. Lindsell is wrong. We simply have a problem wherein honest men see things differently. In these days of instant replays, this should not add to but rather help resolve our problem.

Prepare To Discuss Intelligently

1. Cite the three reasons given for believing in the affirmative position.

2. How do Hebrews 11:32-40 and 2 Corinthians 12:7-11 support the "yes," "no" and "wait" contention?

3. In preparation for class, look up and list as many verses of Scripture as you possibly can which support the two positions in this lesson; namely, (1) God always says "yes"; (2) God sometimes says "no" or "wait."

Source of Quotations

Lindsell, Harold. *When You Pray.* Wheaton, IL: Tyndale House Publishers, Inc., 1969, pp. 76-78. Used by permission.

CHAPTER 8

Problems
(Part II)

BIBLE PORTION TO READ: Hebrews 12:1-15

THIS LESSON is a continuation of the previous one. The problems we are discussing are not by any means intended to discourage prayer; but rather—and hopefully—they will explain the reasons why we have such a difficult time maintaining a consistent practice of prayer. Satan "trembles when we pray"; and you can be sure he will prevent or discourage our praying by any means possible.

Last week we noted that when we look at prayer from God's angle, "nothing is impossible"; but looking at it from the perspective of our experience, there are numerous problems because we so often pray without seeing any apparent effect. We need to read, memorize and claim all of God's promises and to "come boldly" to the throne of grace. We also must recognize our human frailties and make room for the perfect will of God in His answers.

I. Contradictions in Prayer

A. Harold Lindsell, in *When You Pray,* has indicated that we may create "internal contradictions" despite our knowledge of the will of God and of the Scriptures. For example, we read 1 Peter 1:16: "Be ye holy; for I am holy." So we ask God for holiness. We confess every known sin and follow every known rule of the Word of God. However, things seem to become increasingly difficult. Testings and trials—some old and many new —seem to descend upon us, and we pray earnestly for deliverance from these things. We may not have realized that "the trying of your faith worketh patience. But let patience have her perfect work" (James 1:3, 4) is part of the way God is working to answer our prayers for holiness.

Read 1 Peter 1:6 and 7. These words may similarly be the means to the end of holiness resulting in your life. God may say to us, "Which do you want, holiness or comfort?" Usually things of value do not come without great effort, great cost and even suffering. God may need to say "no" to a prayer for comfort in order to say "yes" to holiness. We may need to appropriate Job 23:10.

We have all heard of the girl who prayed for a new doll. Her father purchased the doll; but before he revealed the fact to her, he asked the little girl to give him her old doll. The girl objected because then she would have *no* doll. Finally her father prevailed; and his daughter surrendered the tattered, raggedy doll whereupon she was told to go to her room and look on her bed where the beautiful new doll had been placed. Her father had asked her to give up one thing to get something better. She was in "heaviness" for a while, but "afterward" it yielded peace and joy. Might not God do the same?

Sometimes we create an internal conflict which makes it impossible for God to answer all aspects of our prayers. Therefore, we pray, "Thy will be done."

B. Also, there are "external contradictions." We can mention many of these.

For example, two Christians—both qualified—apply for the same job. How can God say "yes" to both individuals?

A Christian boy prays that his team will win while his buddy, who goes to another school, prays for victory for his team. When the teams play each other, God cannot answer both boys.

A picnic elicits a great deal of prayer for fair weather, but a diligent Christian farmer with a pump broken down prays for rain. How can God send fair weather and rain at the same time?

How can two men running for the same office on opposing party tickets both win?

How can God reconcile the individual desires of a church full of people in calling a pastor?

C. The problem of chastening (Heb. 12:3-15). Frequently in the training of our children, we refuse their requests or discipline them for disobedience, indolence or carelessness. Sometimes we require them to go to bed or get up or practice piano, any of which is not at all to the liking of the child. All of this is chastening or chastisement as mentioned in Hebrews 12. All this is literally "child training," which in verse 11 is described as not "joyous, but grievous." However, afterward it is said to yield "the peaceable fruit of righteousness unto them which are exercised thereby."

Suppose that we pray for easy paths, devoid of such training; and we do so despite our declarations of unfairness, lack of love or even harshness—whether on the part of God or parent—and our prayer is not answered. Then shall we quit praying, run away from home or go about in a morose, despondent mood? Or shall we recognize the possibility that age, experience and—in God's case—infinite wisdom and love are working to make us mature, obedient and righteous? How many thousands are now able to look back and thank

God and parents for the "child training" which at the time was grievous, not joyous!

When contradictions exist, those which are known or unknown, understood or not understood, we cannot conclude that the will of God has been thwarted or that we were not in the will of God when we prayed. We must rather pray, "Thy will be done," and wait to see what God's will is, although we thought we knew when we prayed.

II. The When and How of Prayer

It may be unnecessary—certainly it is trite—to say that God determines when and how prayer will be answered. We can ask God and request the time, place and method; but these things are in God's hands. James reminds us to be careful about our own plans, much less telling God which day, which way and how to go about answering our petitions (James 4:13). Numerous Biblical examples follow:

A. *Joseph* (Gen. 37:5-10) knew, because of the vision God gave him, that his parents and brothers would bow down to him. He did not know when or how; but he very properly could pray that it would come to pass. His brothers hated him and possibly prayed it never would occur. How and when it was accomplished took quite a while; but in Genesis 45:8 Joseph could say, "So now it was not you that sent me hither, but God," when his brothers knelt before him in Egypt during the famine. God accomplished His own purpose—now recognized by Jacob, Joseph and his brothers—and certainly accepted as answered prayer.

2. *Moses* (Exod. 17:5, 6) was told to smite a rock out of which water flowed for the people of Israel and their cattle. Later on (Num. 20:8) he was commanded to speak to the rock, but he presumed to strike the rock as before. Too often we insist that God perform His works the same way He did before because we have made request of Him again. However, He may choose to act differently another time.

A pastor had sold a house easily after praying about it and listing it in the daily newspaper. On another occasion, he followed the same pattern. However, weeks passed; and after much anguish and inconvenience, he sold the second house at a loss. The trauma of an apparent contradiction was not easily overcome until he realized that nothing requires God to repeat Himself.

One of our most frequent problems is "too much month at the end of the money." We confidently claim Philippians 4:19. Now God can answer our prayer in at least four ways: (1) He can send us some extra money; (2) He can give us another job that makes more money; (3) He can give us an extra job to make additional money or (4) we can reduce the budget. If God chooses to have us do the latter, we may well be disappointed; but did God fail to answer Philippians 4:19?

C. *Jesus* even used two different methods to open the eyes of the blind. Matthew 9:27-30 records the prayer of two blind men. Jesus touched their eyes and said: "According to your faith be it unto you"; and they saw. In John 9:1-7 He put clay on another blind man's eyes and told him to wash in the Pool of Siloam. The man obeyed, and he came seeing. Do we have a problem, or is the Son of God free to use the time and method He may desire?

D. *At Lazarus' tomb* (John 11:19-44) several things happened. Jesus had delayed answering the petition to come and heal Lazarus, and the sisters complained (v. 21). Jesus commanded that the tomb be opened, and the sisters objected (vv. 38, 39). So often we try to tell Jesus in our prayers what to do, when and how to do it. We need the instruction of verse 40. Divine delays are not denials.

In Luke 7:11-18 Jesus touched the bier of the widow's son of Nain; and the dead arose. In Mark 5:21-43, He took the daughter of Jairus by the hand and spoke; and she rose from the dead. At the tomb of Lazarus He simply spoke, and Lazarus came forth. When or how God answers is His decision to make, and we must not erroneously doubt or charge God with inconsistency. Paul's prayer for healing (2 Cor. 12:8), Elijah's prayer for rain (1 Kings 18:42-46) and Daniel 10:11-13 record other delays in answered prayer.

We must agree that God does answer prayer but in His own way and His own time and for His own reasons. He is not obligated to answer immediately, and by no means is delay always to be interpreted as denial. Thus we pray, "Thy will be done"; and it both honors God and strengthens faith.

Perhaps we should add a word of reminder that God has two kinds of miracles which He can use in answering prayer: absolute and providential. It must also be pointed out that God more often uses natural phenomena (providential) caused by divine intervention to assume proportions or nature unknown to men and impossible to men. If God chooses to use medicine or surgery in healing, or if He sends money or bread at the hand of a stranger, is it any less an answer to prayer than manna rained from Heaven (absolute)?

III. Rationalization—Feelings and Prayer

One of the distressing by-products of the materialism of our day which has characterized the education and thinking of men for one hundred years is called evolution. This idea was not invented by Charles Darwin, but it has grown apace since he presented rationalization as an explanation for everything. Many of the phenomena in nature have been used, abused and distorted to support the evolutionary hypothesis. Origins, miracles, temperament, etc., do indeed have "logical explanations" and do not require faith, despite Hebrews 11:3 and Colossians 1:16 and 17. Sigmund Freud was of no help when he relegated all our problems to misdirected drives or careless grandparents. Alfred Einstein made it all seem very scholarly with his theories of relativity but without God. Hence we have come to a condition where we have answers for everything, including our failures.

A. We rationalize our way around the will of God by saying, "I'll pray about it." Or we blame Satan for our own laziness or failure. We conclude, "It is not God's will," when really we just don't want to do something. We must be honest enough to face God in prayer; and when we pray "Thy will be done," we must be prepared to face the consequences and do what God asks.

We need to consider that God may want to make changes in our lives in order to answer our prayers. Did a Christian man or woman ever ask God to save the other or change the other so that it would be easier to live in the marriage bond?

Did it ever occur that Ephesians 5:25, 28 and 33 might be the answer for a husband? "Husbands, love your wives"; that is *agape* love. It is not fifty-fifty love, not because all is so lovable. Rather, it is "as Christ also loved the church" — sacrificially, continuously and unfailingly.

Did the wife ever look at verses 22 and 33? She is to "submit" to and "reverence" her husband. Remember that "submit" means "stand in place according to rank" and alongside as an helpmeet. Also, "reverence" here is respect. The wife is to treat her husband like a man—like *the* man she once thought him to be.

Too often the behavior of a wife or husband is a reflection of or response to the behavior of the partner. God may want to answer our prayers by changing us, not others. It is unreasonable to conclude that a person cannot be abnormal if he is a Christian. So, too, it is unreasonable to believe that everything can be solved by prayer alone. Notice that "the rod *and* reproof" are spoken of in Proverbs 29:15. Read 2 Kings 4:18-37 and note that prayer, plus the rod, plus mouth-to-mouth contact brought life to the Shunammite's son.

Prayer is no easy substitute for confession, effort or indolence; but let us believe God and pray. Let us pray and believe God.

B. We often let our feelings govern our praying. That is about the same as letting the assurance of our salvation rest on or be governed by our feelings. When John 10:28 says, "And I give unto them eternal life," it means just that, whether a person feels secure or fearful. Surely Jesus did not feel very good when He prayed in Gethsemane. Prayer is not heard because of our "much speaking" or the nature of our feelings. A wise pastor's wife advised a discouraged young student, "When it is hard to pray, that's the time to pray the hardest."

How many hundreds of people have prayed with great sincerity and emotion, "Lord, let him or her become my life companion," and it did not happen? How many have later married someone else, perfectly sure that God had now answered prayer and often very thankful that the first prayer was not answered!

Most pastors and too many parents could relate tragic stories of cases where the confirmation of the feelings of hearts presented in prayer was not confirmed by God, but the one who prayed went ahead anyway—in impatience or rebellion. Many remorsefully admit that they were tragic decisions to override God's directions or His delays. Too many have decreed, "If I'm wrong, God can stop me," with sorry consequences.

C. Lindsell has referred to "wasted prayers" in which we ask God for things that common sense should tell us not to pray for. Perhaps we should pray with David the words of Psalm 19:13. Many times we "sow wild oats and pray for a crop failure." We know Galatians 6:7 and 8, and it is wasted prayer for us to ask God to reverse the dictum of the Word.

Anyone who has spent much time on airplanes has experienced delays in departure, weather conditions aloft or mechanical difficulties which made it look impossible to make connections with another flight. Important as it may seem, can we expect God to reverse the jet stream so as to speed things up or to double the speed of the plane? Or would that be wasted prayer? Could it be that God has some other thing to teach us?

It is possible for God to help a student recall for an examination material which he has studied, but it is wasted prayer effort if he has not studied. It is possible for God to enable a man to speak another language fluently, but even those who believe in "speaking in tongues" admit that their missionaries must study foreign languages. God apparently does not grant knowledge without study or experience.

We must not blame God if we are irrational when we pray. Prayer is not a substitute for common sense.

Problems in prayer should neither alarm nor defeat us. Rather, they should stimulate and challenge us. Grappling with hard problems, including prayer problems, makes us stronger, more effective and efficient both in prayer and as Christians. Remember, too, that God is not answering prayer simply to substitute spiritual things for other things. God intends to make us a "peculiar people, zealous of good works"; and prayer is a major factor in this process. Every Christian in every age has had problems. We have ours; so let's be on our faces in prayer and trust God.

Prepare To Discuss Intelligently

1. Give the three prerequisites for determining the will of God with or without a "fleece."

2. How should we pray when we feel that God is chastening us?

3. How does the life of Joseph illustrate the wisdom of waiting on God?

4. How does the life of Moses illustrate the danger of not waiting on God?

Source of Quotations

Lindsell, Harold. *When You Pray*. Wheaton, IL: Tyndale House, 1969, pp. 83-86, 92. Used by permission.

CHAPTER 9

A Study of Jesus' Prayer Life

BIBLE PORTION TO READ: Mark 1:21-35

THERE ARE SEVERAL WAYS of learning. One is by reading or hearing instruction or information. Another is by seeing a thing done, and another is by doing it oneself. Many times it takes all three methods; and we may boldly affirm that if we are really to learn to pray, we will need all three.

Certainly we will never find a better teacher than our Lord Jesus Christ, and surely we can find no better source to look for His teaching on prayer, what He did when He prayed and what He has instructed us to do about it than in the New Testament, most especially in the Gospels.

Any good study Bible will suggest the chronology of events in Jesus' life—particularly during the last week of His earthly life, the events on the day of crucifixion and the day of resurrection. Without too much trouble, the same can be done in the matter of Jesus' prayer life.

We have leaned upon S. D. Gordon and his *Quiet Talks on Prayer*. That writer has stated that there are fifteen accounts in the Gospels concerning Jesus' prayers. Matthew mentions three, Mark and John each mention four and Luke mentions eleven. Obviously, there are some duplications among the fifteen recorded instances arranged here in chronological order.

I. At His Baptism

Matthew, Mark and Luke each mentioned the baptism of Jesus; but it was Luke who added in 3:21 and 22, "and praying." We would expect Jesus to pray before He did almost anything. However, is it not significant that at this public declaration of His identification both with sinful man and God, this open demonstration of His obedience to God's plan and will —His inauguration ceremony no less—we should read, "and praying"? Jesus knew that prayer brings power, even the power of the Holy Spirit. S. D. Gordon wrote, "Prayer is power. The time of prayer is the time of power. The place of prayer is the place of power. Prayer is tightening the connections with the divine dynamo so that the power may flow freely without loss or interruption."

Never try to begin anything without prayer. Like modern electronic ignitions, you cannot get started without it.

II. After a Busy Sabbath

Read Mark 1:21-39 and the companion portion in Luke 4:31-44. The Lord Jesus was in Capernaum teaching in the synagogue; He was interrupted by a demon whom He cast out, by the healing of Peter's mother-in-law and by a whole city gathered at the door to be healed of their diseases and demons. He must have been exhausted by the time the people finally left and He had an opportunity to get some rest. On such occasions most of us would feel that we deserved a little extra rest and should be allowed to sleep in the next morning. Or if we did get up early the next morning, it would be to escape the telephone and shoot a round of golf for relaxation.

One cannot condemn such reasoning or practice; but is it not interesting that when everyone else arose the next morning at Peter's in-laws' home—and Jesus

---

A Verse To Memorize

"And when he [Jesus] had sent the multitudes away, he went up into a mountain apart to pray: and when the evening was come, he was there alone" (Matt. 14:23).

---

was not in His room—Peter guessed where He might be found (Mark 1:34-37). He had risen "in the morning . . . a great while before day" to go off by Himself to pray. When Peter found Him, he almost criticized Jesus for leaving the crowds of people who were clamoring for His attention. Peter was so much like the average pastor, the average Christian nowadays! We are caught up in an "activity syndrome" which causes us to feel guilty if we sit down to read or pray or just rest; and it causes us to criticize others who may do so.

"Prayer wonderfully clears the vision; steadies the nerves; defines duty; stiffens the purpose; sweetens and strengthens the spirit. The busier the day for Him, the more surely must the morning appointment be kept," wrote S. D. Gordon (p. 214). Would it not be wise to conclude likewise and spend time, more time, much time with Him at the place of power—even if it means rising early!

III. In Galilee

Probably following the above events (Luke 4:44), Jesus went into Galilee (5:1-16). (Note verse 16.) The inference in this text is that Jesus made a practice of "withdrawing," "retiring" and "getting away" in order to have time to pray.

Another form of the "activity syndrome" is the "work syndrome" which results in some people's becoming "workaholics"! We have a compulsion to be doing some useful thing every moment. Even vacations must be planned to take in everything along the way so that we come home with rolls of film, but utterly exhausted in mind and body. Jesus seems to say "no" to this compulsion. We are not to work all the time but rather work first with a prayer en route for God's blessing. He does not prescribe endless planning and then a season of prayer before blast-off. Jesus seems to suggest that we take time to recharge in the closet, in the wilderness; and the more pressure we must endure, the greater is the need for unhurried prayer.

IV. In the Mountains

Jesus was now in the second year of His ministry. The leaders of the people, the scribes and Pharisees were continually criticizing (Luke 6:1-5), complaining and opposing (Luke 6:6-11). Read verse 12 to see what Jesus did. This turned out to be the night before He chose the twelve disciples "whom he named apostles"; and when this group came down from the mountain, He went about healing the multitude who had come to hear Him and to be healed (Luke 6:17, 18).

How many times when something important is pending, something unpleasant will come up to make problems. It could be anything from having a little boy fall down and get dirty as you leave the house for Sunday School—and you are a teacher who needs to be there early—to a report of a tragedy or a disgruntled member just before you step into the pulpit. Satan's timing is often very effective. That migraine headache or dead battery seems often to occur.

Can we learn a lesson from Jesus? He sought out a time to be alone with God. He couldn't stop in the middle of things either; but He counted that time of prayer more important than physical comfort, and it was necessary for the continuance of the ministry to which He had been called.

V. Another Mountain

Matthew 14:1-14 tells us that Jesus had just received

word of the murder of John the Baptist. This news—
with its ominous forebodings—laid heavily upon the
heart of Jesus; so He went with His disciples across
the Sea of Galilee to be alone. However, He arrived
on the other side to find a crowd awaiting. His great
heart of compassion welled up and overflowed His
own grief, and "he healed their sick" (v. 14). By evening the disciples reported the desperate condition of
many who were present. Most of the crowd had no food
all day. We know of the miracle of the loaves and fishes
and of the 5,000 plus whom He fed (Matt. 14:15-21).

Then Jesus sent the disciples back whence they had
come, and "he went up into a mountain apart to pray"
(14:23). This was another night on another mountain,
a night preceded by great pressures, thus requiring
communion with God more than rest or food.

"How much more [of power and everything else]
there must have been in prayer as He understood and
practiced it than many of His disciples to-day know"
(S. D. Gordon).

VI. With His Disciples

In Luke 9:18-21 we read, "And it came to pass, as
he was alone praying, his disciples were with him."
Prayer has this remarkable faculty of rendering one
all alone with God, even in the midst of a crowd or
confusion. However, in this case, it seems more likely
that this was one of those wonderful occasions when
a group of believers—no matter how many there might
be—were alone with God, wrapped in the sweet bond
of faith and prayer.

Perhaps Jesus was trying to draw His disciples into
the sacred inner precincts of secret prayer. They
would need to know how to pray for and with one
another when He would be gone. They would need to
remember this precious fellowship. "And there is no
fellowship among men to be compared with fellowship
in prayer" (Gordon).

VII. Transfigured While Praying

Matthew 17 and Mark 9 record the Transfiguration scene; but again it was Luke who added the details of Luke 9:27-36: "He took Peter and John and James, and went up into a mountain to pray. And as he prayed, the fashion of his countenance was altered," transfigured before them (vv. 28, 29)! By His side stood Moses who, having spent time on a mountain with God, came down from the mountain with the glory of God on his face.

Without going into the significance of the Transfiguration, may we not properly deduce that time spent in God's presence—in the light of His Word—with open faces turned up to God in prayer, will do for us what it did for Moses and for Jesus!

Perhaps it shines on our faces too! May it not be that Paul was thinking like this when he wrote 2 Corinthians 3:18? Might it be possible that if we would get alone with God in prayer often enough and long enough, with eyes undimmed by self-seeking or prejudice, we should more and more bear in our faces the very likeness of Christ? What a glorious thought—transfigured while praying!

VIII. Ejaculatory Prayer and Praise

The significance of Luke 10:21 is found in the spontaneity of the praise which came from Jesus' lips. So intimate was His relationship, His association and His consciousness of His Father's presence that He could speak to God without any hindrance or hesitation—instantly, immediately and freely.

Having sent out the disciples two-by-two and hearing their glowing reports as they returned, Jesus simply burst into a prayer of praise and thanksgiving. This can be our experience as well. In Dr. Viggo Olsen's book *Daktar*, did you pick up the little ejaculation, "Thank You, Father," spoken with this same spontaneity on almost any occasion wherein God's good hand had been seen?

IX. Teach Us To Pray

Again Jesus was with His disciples. They were certainly praying men, and Jesus had already talked to them about prayer; but they witnessed a different tone, power, force and secret in His praying. Therefore, they requested, "Lord, teach us to pray [like that]," for He had just concluded praying (Luke 11:1).

Prayer is a fine art which is developed by practice. The instructor simply sets the lesson before the pupil and sends the pupil home to practice. It is to be hoped that this lesson will set the score before us; and as we watch Jesus pray, it will inspire us to go home and practice.

X. Jesus at Lazarus' Tomb

It will be interesting to read John 11:1-44 to see if you can find where Jesus prayed. Prior to going to Bethany (v. 16) Jesus only commented on the fact that Lazarus was asleep and it was His intent to waken him. In His conversation with Mary and Martha there was the testing of their faith but no evidence of prayer. In fact, the only prayer is another of the ejaculatory type (vv. 41, 42). (He gave thanks for a prayer that we didn't hear.)

Evidently the intimacy Jesus shared with the Father made possible prayer that no one heard. Because none heard His petition, He here expressed His thanks to God so that Mary, Martha and the others would realize that God hears and answers prayer and that Omnipotence is at the disposal of the one who prays. Also, it is so that we may know that secret prayer avails even to quicken the dead in trespasses and sins.

XI. Preparation for Gethsemane

Two or three days before Calvary, following that so-called triumphal entry into Jerusalem, the shadow of the cross began to loom ominously before Jesus. In the contemplation of the horrible prospect of becoming sin for us, we hear our Lord pray, "Now is my soul

77

troubled" (John 12:27). To this author it seems that the next phrase is a question: "Shall I pray, Father save Me from this hour?" Then with an understood negative response He prayed (vv. 27, 28), "For this cause came I into the world." (See John 18:37.) "Father, glorify thy name," Christ prayed; and as soon as He uttered it, the answer came, "I have both glorified it, and will glorify it again."

Again there was that tremendous intimacy between the Father and the Son which produced an immediate answer. May our walk be so close, our motives in prayer so pure and the assurance in our hearts so perfect that we too can receive such answers.

XII. In the Upper Room

Jesus was in the upper room with the disciples (Luke 22:14-30). The Lord's Supper was instituted; the betrayal was announced and the question of preferment in the Kingdom was discussed. It was probably at this point that Jesus gave them the example of humility recorded in John 13:2-20 and added the words of Luke 22:31-34. Jesus prayed for Peter by name!

Much more wonderful: Jesus is still praying for His own by name! Hebrews 7:25 assures us of this.

How can we for whom the Son of God prays by name possibly fail?

XIII. The High Priestly Prayer

This is indeed the Lord's prayer, the prayer He Himself prayed rather than the one He taught His disciples to pray.

Since we consider both prayers—Matthew 6:9-15 and this one in John 17:1-26—we will list only this latter prayer at this point and let you look for the treatment elsewhere in this text.

XIV. In Gethsemane

Jesus' prayer in the Garden is found in Matthew 26:36-46; Mark 14:32-42 and Luke 22:39-46. Now He was face to face with the specter He saw in John 12 (point XI). He Who knew no sin now began to realize what it meant to "become sin." He Who could not die began to feel the clammy hand; He Who loved because He is love began to feel the agony of being forsaken, unloved and hated. And His mind and body were strained until His agony pressed from His forehead "great drops [clots] of blood."

There He prayed thrice; and having found assurance and victory somewhere in that awful night, He prayed, "Thy will be done"; and to the disciples who slept, He said, "Let us be going." Then He led them forth to the betrayal, arrest, trial, scourging and the cross—victorious through prayer! Lord, teach *me* to pray like that!

XV. On the Cross

Of the famous "seven last words" Jesus spoke from the cross, three were prayers:

Luke 23:34 gives Jesus' words as they drove the nails through His hands and feet. Matthew 27:46 and Luke 23:46 report other ejaculatory prayers.

So the prayer life and the prayer habits of the Lord Jesus serve forever to set us an example that we should follow in His steps.

Prepare To Discuss Intelligently

1. How would you define "ejaculatory" prayer?
2. What did Jesus mean by inferring that Lazarus was only asleep?
3. What three ways do we learn, and how does each one apply to prayer?
4. Explain how the "activity syndrome" and the "work syndrome" hinder prayer.

Source of Quotations

Gordon, S. D. *Quiet Talks on Prayer*. Old Tappan, NJ: Fleming H. Revell Co., 1904, pp. 209-234. Used by permission.

CHAPTER 10

Powerful Pray-ers

BIBLE PORTIONS TO READ: Psalms 4:1-8; 77:1-20

HAROLD LINDSELL, in his chapter "The Power of Prayer" (*When You Pray*, chap. VII), approaches the matter of power in prayer as a phenomenon in nature or life which we can explore from several angles. For example, we can approach prayer as Albert Einstein, namely: (1) From the *hypothetical viewpoint.* Einstein had no facts with which to begin when he began to study the theory of relativity. By experimentation he had to endeavor to find evidence which would support his ideas. When he was satisfied, he expressed his theory in the now famous formula $E = MC^2$. Most of us who are laymen in the field of science—physics, particularly—still have a very inadequate grasp of relativity except to know that the atomic bomb and numerous nuclear power plants demonstrate that it is true and that it works.

A second form of research—like Newton's law of gravity—is the reverse of Einstein's approach. Newton began to study what men had always known: that "what goes up must come down." This method might be called the (2) *ex post facto method.* The facts were here and observable. All Newton did was to figure out why things always fell to earth and how fast they fell.

He did this, and we can scientifically adjust to the laws of gravity.

A third type of research might be called (3) *conditional research* in which we begin with what has been known and proven and theorize as to what may happen if we combine certain known factors. Most of modern research is in this latter area although we continue to explore pure theory in fields of pure science.

Our purpose in this lesson is to suggest that God has given us factual statements concerning prayer which —whether we understand them or not—have been proven to work. Hence we can move from observable phenomena based on sure promises to workable combinations in our own lives. We will attempt to accomplish this by citing a number of cases in God's Word where men and women of God prayed and received answers. Not only is this to encourage us to believe the promises but also to emulate the examples of powerful pray-ers.

It will not be our effort to quote every verse or cite every instance recorded where Abraham and others prayed. Neither will it be our endeavor to list every person or prayer recorded in Scripture. We will notice briefly, and we trust effectively, the observable results of power in prayer in each person; and hope to encourage—even challenge—believers to go and do likewise.

I. Abraham Was a Powerful Pray-er (Gen. 18:1-33)

In Genesis 18:1-33 three angelic messengers came to Abraham. Whether or not Abraham recognized them as angels is questionable; but keeping Hebrews 13:2 in mind, it is well to make the point that communion and prayer go together. It may have been simple hospitality which caused Abraham to feed and fellowship with his guests who turned out to be angels, perhaps even theophanies (visible manifestations of the Godhead). Certainly, when we intentionally come to God in prayer, it would seem very wise for us first to spend some time in communion, fellowship and medi-

Verses To Memorize

"But know that the LORD hath set apart him
that is godly for himself: the LORD will hear
when I call unto him. Stand in awe, and sin not:
commune with your own heart upon your bed,
and be still. Selah" (Ps. 4:3, 4).

tation with God before we engage in prayer. It would
seem entirely possible that our tendency to dash into and
out of God's presence when we pray may actually be a
deterrent to answered prayer.

Then when the planned visitation of judgment upon
Sodom and Gomorrah was revealed to Abraham—
which judgment would affect the lives of perhaps
thousands, among them Abraham's nephew Lot and
his family—Abraham "stood yet before the LORD"
(v. 22). Perhaps Abraham was in shock as we refer to
the effects of such an announcement, but it seems more
likely that he was continuing the spirit of communion
while his spirit pondered these grave matters. He did
not panic; he did not fall on his face and pound on the
ground and hysterically plead with God. It would
appear that he calmly, reverently and persistently besought God not less than six times for Sodom. Evidently he did not even mention Lot by name.

In spite of Abraham's faith, importunity and persistence in interceding prayer, he prevailed only to
the extent that Lot, his two daughters and—for a dis-
appointing moment—his wife were rescued. Powerful
prayer by a powerful pray-er was nevertheless demonstrated. Communion and persistence pay off in effective,
intercessory prayer. Recite our memory verses, Psalm
4:3, 4: "But know that the LORD hath set apart him
that is godly for himself: the LORD will hear when I call
unto him. Stand in awe, and sin not: commune with
your own heart upon your bed, and be still. Selah."

II. Jacob Was a Powerful Pray-er (Gen. 32:1-32)

Genesis 32:9-12 records the prayer of Jacob as he faced the prospect of meeting his brother Esau upon his return to Canaan. Note only that Jacob reminded God of His promises and His directives and requested protection and preservation in order that the promises of God should not be brought into disrepute. Surely Jacob was afraid; but rather than attribute cowardly self-preservation to Jacob, let us emulate the boldness and faith in the promises upon which his prayer is based. (See Psalms 42 and 43.)

In verses 22-32 we have the familiar account of Jacob's struggle with the angel. Dr. William Orr, in *How To Pray,* said that here was a picture of prayer in action. What was happening that night was first of all God's faithful dealing with recalcitrant Jacob until he absolutely came to the end of himself and was forced to depend wholly on God. The story concerns Jacob's "perseverance in prayer . . . holding on to God . . . until God blessed him."

This author confesses uncertainty about this incident, but he will agree that Jacob's persistence at this time of crisis resulted in a transformation of the man from merely "Jacob the Supplanter" into "Israel—a Prince of God."

Scofield has commented that Jacob is the natural, human name of both the man and the nation while Israel is the spiritual name in both cases. Often such a climactic experience of wrestling with God in prayer is found to be the turning point in the lives of a host of other godly men. In fact, probably most men who have attained historical attention have been men of prayer who had such experiences.

III. Hannah Was a Powerful Pray-er (1 Sam. 1:1-28)

In these days when the Equal Rights Amendment to our national constitution is being voted upon by the several states and when the "liberation" movement—especially as it refers to women—is getting great attention, it might be well to suggest that Hannah is an example of a woman who obtained her heart's desire through prayer (1 Sam. 1:1-28).

Hannah's request was based on the fact that she had no children. She evidently would not agree with many young women nowadays who seem to be willing to go to great lengths to prevent the birth of children, even to murder, popularly referred to as abortion. She believed that "children are an heritage of the LORD: and the fruit of the womb is his reward" (Ps. 127:3). See also Genesis 33:5 where Jacob refers to "the children which God hath graciously given thy servant." Also Rachel, the wife of Jacob, grieved that she had no children and evidently prayed; for we find in Genesis 30:22 that "God remembered Rachel, and God hearkened to her, and opened her womb." In Luke 1: 5-25 Elisabeth became the mother of John the Baptist after long years of prayer following the lead of Sarah.

Without straining the Scriptures or the experience of these women, it seems evident that women who pray in the will of God are heard and receive answers. Hannah also prayed earnestly "in bitterness of soul, and prayed unto the LORD, and wept sore" (1 Sam. 1:10). Intensity, importunity and persistence again are seen as significant elements in the lives of those who pray successfully.

Would God that every mother could say of her child, "I prayed and asked my child of God," even though she might not call him Samuel, "asked of God." Would God that every Christian mother might make her children her constant prayer even to dedicating them to God for His service as did Hannah with Samuel.

IV. Elijah Was a Powerful Pray-er (1 Kings 17:1—19:21)

One of the outstanding pray-ers is Elijah whose record is found mostly in 1 Kings 17:1—19:21. Most significant is the incident regarding the son of the widow of Zarephath (1 Kings 17:8-24), especially verses 17-24. The child died, and the distraught mother bitterly reproached Elijah. Taking the dead child to his own room, Elijah prayed with great boldness in words like these, "Why has this child died?" It is evident that this is not the usual plea for explanations; but rather it was a bold challenge to God, indicating the strength of Elijah's faith. This is further demonstrated by the intensity of this man's praying who, in the act of prayer, concentrated on the intercession and supplication for this child and the request for a miracle.

In a similar situation Elisha, the successor to Elijah (2 Kings 4:18-35, especially verses 33-35), restored life to another child following the example of Elijah. Again the intensity of the prayer, accompanied by the "hand-to-hand, mouth-to-mouth" contact, is emphasized. How to explain the details may be difficult; but that personal, intimate, intense intercession, supplication, boldness and faith are certainly not difficult to deduce as important to powerful pray-ers.

Again let us turn back to Elijah and Mount Carmel and the four hundred prophets of Baal (1 Kings 18:17-39) which story we know well. Note that after the utter failure of the prophets of Baal, Elijah prepared an altar and a sacrifice, the details of which make a lesson in themselves. Then he prayed (vv. 36, 37), "LORD God of Abraham, Isaac, and of Israel, let it be known this day that thou art God. . . . Hear me, O LORD, hear me, that this people may know that thou art the LORD God."

The glory of God is a proper incentive in prayer. This is the exact opposite of the "consume it upon your lusts" (James 4:3) kind of praying. Elijah could pray with confidence because the answer would magnify the power and glory of God. This is a good way to live ("Whether therefore ye eat, or drink, or whatsoever ye do, do all to the glory of God"—1 Cor. 10:31) and a powerful way to pray.

Space will not permit dealing with Daniel who in

chapter 2:17 and 18 of the book that bears his name en-
listed his friends to pray with him for wisdom (James
1:5) whereby we learn about the power of united prayer.
Also note Daniel 6:10 and 11 where Daniel "prayed,
and gave thanks . . . making supplication" before God.
As a result, he was delivered from the den of lions; and
a powerful witness for God was effected. Courage,
faithfulness and diligence as being marks of a powerful pray-er are seen.

Then there is the account of Jonah 2:1-10 giving the
prayer from the belly of the fish. Jonah was not on
praying ground; certainly he was in a precarious
condition. However, no one is ever out of reach of God
in prayer.

V. David Was a Powerful Pray-er (Ps. 51:1-19)

The Psalms are full of David's prayers. We call
your attention particularly to Psalm 51, and we urge
you to read 2 Samuel 11:1—12:25, especially verses 12
and 13 of chapter 12. This Psalm describes the prayer
of confession, remorse and repentance and the resultant forgiveness and cleansing of David in the matter
of his great sin with Bath-sheba. We know 1 John 1:9;
but too often, like David, we cover up and shut the
door and wallow in remorse or self-pity instead of
boldly, openly and sincerely coming to the throne of
grace to plead the blood in humble repentance and
faith. Great pray-ers maintain themselves by honesty
with God in the matter of their own sins. Read the
Psalm several times, and note the attitudes manifest
and the nature of David's petitions.

VI. A Publican and a Thief Were Powerful Pray-ers
(Luke 18:9-14; 23:39-43)

Very similar to the last instance—except that it
comes at the other end of the social scale—is the case
of the publican in Luke 18:9-14. The contrast between
the powerless, proud Pharisee's prayer and that of the

poor, penitent publican is easy to notice. In verse 14 Jesus made the application by telling us that pride and self-righteousness are barriers to prayer, but humility and penitence are frequently suggested to sinners who seek salvation; and this is only proper. The prayer of faith thus addressed to the Lord Jesus Christ will always avail for forgiveness and cleansing. This prayer is the essence of believing in John 5:24, confessing (Rom. 10:9, 10) and calling (Rom. 10:13).

The scene on Calvary, as recorded in Luke 23, includes the prayer of desperation on the part of one of the two thieves who were crucified with Christ (23:39-43). Surely no more radical reversal or genuine repentance is noted in Scripture than this account. Far from recommending "deathbed conversions," it is nevertheless important to know that such are possible. The desperate, agonizing, exceedingly brief prayer, "Lord, remember me when thou comest into thy kingdom," speaks volumes. Of course, verses 40 and 41 reveal the first evidences of a change of mind resulting in a change of action. This is a good definition for repentance; but the prayer itself is indicative of belief in the deity of Christ, for the thief addressed Christ as "Lord." It manifests some understanding of the purposes of God by reference to "thy kingdom"; and it reaches out by faith in the plea "remember me," evidencing confidence in the resurrection. Read again Romans 10:9 and 10, and pray that powerful prayer; or if you have already done so, be ready to help the sinner you meet to receive the Lord Jesus Christ by praying in this way.

VII. Cornelius Was a Powerful Pray-er

We should take time to look at Peter's prayer in Acts 9:36-42 where the powerful prayer of Peter restored life to Tabitha-Dorcas. The result of this was that "many believed in the Lord." The age of miraculous healings in order to convince unbelievers is past, but it is not so with the age of miracles. A few more men like Peter who had the kind of faith he had would move some modern mountains; but where are those kind of pray-ers?

So, too, we should look at Paul in Acts 16:25 and the resultant conversion of a whole family. Also read Acts 28:8 and the healing of Publius' father; but we will turn only to Acts 10:1-48 to consider Cornelius, passing by Peter's experience on the rooftop.

Cornelius, a Gentile, but a believer and a pray-er (Acts 10:1, 2) had a word from God in verses 4-6. The result was that God had to send a special message to convince Peter that Gentiles were now eligible to receive blessings which were hitherto limited to Israel and also eligible to accept Christ even as were the Jews. This done (vv. 44-48), Cornelius and evidently his household received Jesus Christ and gave the then acceptable evidence of conversion and valid faith, i.e., speaking in tongues.

The point is that anyone can be a powerful pray-er, even Gentiles—even Jews—anyone!

Prepare To Discuss Intelligently

1. What would have happened if Abraham had continued to intercede in Genesis 18?

2. What is a theophany?

3. Suggest a reason why God changed Jacob's name as indicated by comparing the meaning of that name and the name "Israel."

4. What do 1 Kings 18:36 and 37 reveal as a valid motive and incentive in prayer?

5. Using Psalm 51, list some aspects of valid prayer.

Source of Quotations

Lindsell, Harold. "The Power of Prayer," *When You Pray*. Wheaton, IL: Tyndale House Publishers, Inc., 1969. Used by permission.

CHAPTER 11

Prayer—Worry—Healing

BIBLE PORTION TO READ: Psalm 73:1-28

ONE OF THE OLDEST PROBLEMS for believers
is the problem of suffering: "Why do the righteous
suffer?"

Opinions differ widely on why and what are the
causes and cures. They vary from statements that it is
not God's will for Christians to suffer, to the idea that
the body is of and for the earth and therefore has little
spiritual significance. As a result, we can "eat, and
. . . drink, and . . . be merry"; and the sooner we can
get out of the body the better. Certainly the latter is
not true, and probably the former is likewise not true
or only partially true.

I. Prayer and Worry

It is of great concern to earnest Christians that some
of God's choice servants suffer deprivation, opposition, torture and death, while some carnal, worldly believers—even many unbelievers—prosper. Read Psalm
73:1-15, but do not forget to read verses 16-19 also.
That Christian people today should share the common
ills of man is perhaps not strange; but that Christians,
like unbelievers, should spend hundreds of dollars for
sleeping pills and tranquilizers; that they should suffer
from ulcers, gastritis and psychosomatic ailments, is

a proper cause for concern. Why should worry, vexation of spirit, phobias, nervous indigestion, etc., plague Christians?

Jesus said, "Peace I leave with you, my peace I give unto you. . . . Let not your heart be troubled, neither let it be afraid" (John 14:27).

"These things I have spoken unto you, that in me ye might have peace. In the world ye shall have tribulation: but be of good cheer; I have overcome the world" (John 16:33).

It seems apparent that Jesus made a distinction between the world which has no peace and believers who do—or should or can—yet so many don't. How can we explain this, and what is the remedy? Norman B. Harrison, *His in a Life of Prayer*, chapter IV, suggests the following:

A. Why We Worry

1. *Because we have the habit.* The contingencies of life are so numerous that unless we are very careful, we will begin to worry about them. There is no end of subjects about which to be worried. Once we get the habit, we become more addicted as time goes on. Finally sleeplessness, ulcers, breakdown and depression result.

2. *We worry because others worry.* It is contagious. The world worries and has ample reason to do so. The spirit of fear prevailing in the world is picked up by Christians. The world quips, "If you are not worried, you don't understand things." Likewise they tell us "Ignorance is bliss." However, both are wrong. The sense of impending judgment causes "fear of the things coming upon the earth"; but Christians who, according to John 5:24, "shall not come into condemnation" should have nothing about which to worry. "He hath said, I will never leave thee, nor forsake thee. So that we may boldly say, The Lord is my helper, and I will not fear what man shall do unto me" (Heb. 13:5, 6).

Let us not allow the infection of the world to invade our hearts.

3. *We worry because we do not believe God.* Have we never read Matthew 6:25-34 where Jesus assured us of our Heavenly Father's care? This assurance does not invite indolence, but it does remove the need to worry about simple necessities. The remark, "O ye of little faith," would seem to be a rebuke for worry.

But then Jesus added in essence: "Don't worry. Take no thought about all these things." Three times "all these things" are mentioned in Matthew 6:32 and 33. The first time (a) He said that Gentiles, unbelievers and the heathen worry about "all these things." In Ephesians 4:17 and 18 Paul told us not to "walk . . . as other Gentiles walk." It would appear to be a rather serious matter to worry since it says that we either do not know God and His promises or we do not believe Him.

Again (b) Jesus has assured us that "your heavenly Father knoweth that ye have need of 'all these things.'" Dare we charge God with ignorance or unconcern as did the disciples in the storm: "Carest thou not that we perish?" In the third instance (c) Jesus gives us the formula, "Seek ye first the kingdom of God, and his righteousness; and all these things shall be added unto you." In other words, "Therefore, don't worry." Worry is a declaration of lack of faith and is an insult to our Heavenly Father.

B. Why Not Worry?

1. *Because it is harmful.* You cannot find a single

benefit produced by worry. You can list one hundred bad things which worry produces, but you cannot list one which is helpful.

The fruit of the Holy Spirit being in us is "love, joy, peace, longsuffering, gentleness, goodness, faith, meekness, temperance [self-control]" (Gal. 5:22, 23). Unless these things are in us, something is wrong. Either we are not saved or we are not trusting the leading of the Holy Spirit.

A person may deprive himself of Heaven by worry to say nothing of depriving himself of the peace Christ came to give.

2. *Because it is harmful to your friends.* Just as you can catch worry from your unsaved friends, they can catch it from you. If Christians "crack-up," "break down" or "fall apart" as do unbelievers, the world may well conclude that we have nothing that will help them. It is a serious consideration! How many people who are your friends are still lost because when you are with them, you spend the time sharing your worries instead of sharing your faith!

3. *Because it hurts our Heavenly Father.* Read again Matthew 6:25-34. Read Matthew 14:22-32 and note the tearful rebuke Jesus leveled at Peter, "O thou of little faith, wherefore didst thou doubt [worry]?" Don't you think that Jesus was grieved with Thomas in John 20:24-29 when He said, "Be not faithless [a worrier], but believing [one who believes and trusts]"?

C. How Not To Worry

1. *Pray according to Philippians 4:6 and 7:* "Be careful [full of care, anxious, worried] for nothing [nothing]; but in every thing by prayer and supplication with thanksgiving let your requests be made known unto God. And the peace of God, which passeth all understanding, shall keep [protect by a military guard] your hearts and minds through Christ Jesus."

Here it is in plain English, "Do not worry about anything, but pray about everything."

2. *"Casting [unload] all your care upon him; for he careth for you"* (1 Pet. 5:7). Plainly, will you insist on worry or trust, fear or faith, care or prayer? It is as though the Lord was saying, "Make a choice; give it *all* to Me or carry it *all* yourself." We cannot trust and doubt at the same time; we cannot pray and worry at the same time.

3. *Stop looking at your problems and start "looking unto Jesus"* (Heb. 12:2). This is a recognized principle in psychology, but it was here in the Word all the time. We must stop looking at, dwelling upon, worrying about "all these things" and then:

"Turn your eyes upon Jesus,
Look full in His wonderful face;
And the things of earth will grow strangely dim
In the light of His glory and grace."

4. *Stop depending on things, and concentrate on the person of God and the work of Christ for you.* Isaiah 26:3 promises, "Thou wilt keep him in perfect peace, whose mind is stayed on [focused on, concentrated on] thee; because he trusteth in thee." Stop looking at big problems, circumstances and needs; and begin contemplating the greatness of God and the price paid for your redemption. Remember Romans 8:31 and 32: "If God be for us, who can be against us? He that spared not his own Son, but delivered him up for us all, how shall he not with him also freely give us *all* things?"

5. *Read and obey Psalm 37:1-8:*

a. "Fret not," which means don't worry.

b. "Trust in the LORD." You cannot stand up and sit down at the same time; neither can you trust and worry simultaneously.

c. "Delight thyself also in the LORD." Set your mind upon the Lord and His good gifts bestowed on you personally, subjectively.

d. "Commit thy way unto the LORD"; and let Him take care of the outward, objective circumstances.

e. "Rest in the Lord, and wait patiently for him."

93

You expect to wait for food or medicine to take effect; therefore, give God a little time and remember that "all things work together for good" (Rom 8:28).

f. "Fret not thyself . . . because of the man who bringeth wicked devices to pass"; fret not about getting revenge. "Vengeance is mine; I will repay, saith the Lord" (Rom. 12:19). Prayer is the secret to a life without worry. "For it is God which worketh in you both to will and to do of his good pleasure" (Phil. 2:13).

II. Prayer and Healing

This subject is the basis for a great deal of confusion among Christians. Some declare that healing is in the atonement; hence it comes with our salvation. Therefore, a Christian should not be ill; and if ever he becomes ill, he can claim healing as part of what was purchased for him at Calvary.

Other Christians feel that illness and death are part of life and should be faced honestly and prayerfully. We do not intend to become involved in debate on either side; but following the lead of Dr. John R. Rice in his big book on prayer, look at the place of prayer in the matter of healing.

Whether worry or illness is the problem, the believer must not follow the pattern of the world. We have become a generation of "pill-poppers" with bathroom medicine closets filled with every kind of remedy for every imaginable ailment. Christians frequently run for a pill and seldom "take it to the Lord in prayer." Is it not a poor testimony to carry a purse full of pills and depend on them instead of carrying a heart full of God's promises and claim them in prayer for "all our need"?

Let us look at this subject sensibly as well as Scripturally.

A. Some Sickness Is Caused by Sin

Anything from pickles and ice cream eaten at a picnic to pizza eaten late at night can be the cause for acute indigestion. Such ailments have no necessary connection with believing, but they are related to the use of common sense. Ignorance, lack of good judgment or indiscretion should be treated with common sense. In such cases prayer is proper, but God is likely to remind you to avoid such practices rather than miraculously removing the consequences.

Such practices for a Christian may very well be considered sinful since our bodies, being the temples of the Holy Spirit, should be treated properly; and when they are abused, they warrant the application of 1 John 1:9. Numerous Biblical examples of illness caused by sin can be cited. Note the following instances:

Miriam (Num. 12:1-16)

Jeroboam (1 Kings 13:1-4)

Gehazi (2 Kings 5:20-27)

Uzziah (2 Chron. 26:16-21)

Herod (Acts 12:20-23)

Ananias and Sapphira (Acts 5:1-10)

Careless, carnal Christians (1 Cor. 11:30-32)

Jesus indicated that sin was involved (John 5:14; Mark 2:5-11).

All of these indicate that we need to consider the possibility that sin may be involved in our illnesses; and if it is, we must confess it and seek the healing which God promises. James 5:15 and 16 urge that Christians can and should pray for healing of this sort and help one another in such situations, "And the prayer of faith shall save the sick, and the Lord shall raise him up; and if he have committed sins, they shall be forgiven him . . . pray one for another, that ye may be healed."

B. Some Sickness Is Caused by Satan

The classic example is that of Job whose sickness was the direct result of Satanic attack (Job 1:1—2:8). Jesus healed a woman (Luke 13:10-17) of whom He said: "And ought not this woman, being a daughter of Abraham [the equivalent of a believer], whom Satan hath bound, lo, these eighteen years, be loosed?" In 2

Corinthians 12:7 Paul's thorn in the flesh was identified as "the messenger of Satan."

That "Satan is alive and well on planet earth" is not now held up to ridicule as has been the case for years. We are now in danger of playing into the hands of Satan by becoming obsessed with interest in or fear of Satan. Christians must remember that Satan is a defeated enemy. He is still "the god of this world" (2 Cor. 4:4), but his power and dominion are limited by God. "Greater is he that is in you, than he that is in the world" (1 John 4:4). We ought to pray earnestly that God would keep us from the Evil One; that He would reinforce our lives and testimonies with "the shield of faith, wherewith ye shall be able to quench all the fiery darts of the wicked" (Eph. 6:16) and pray for one another. Be very careful about giving much time to the many cults, mysteries, Ouija boards, fortune tellers, zodiac horoscopes, etc. Keep your mind set on things above, and pray for deliverance from and protection from Satanic temptation, influence or oppression.

C. It Is Not Always God's Will To Heal

The great Dr. Reuben A. Torrey in his book on divine healing reminds us that many men of God were sick without attributing their illnesses to sin, carnality, Satan or anything else; e.g., 2 Kings 13:14-17 where Elisha lay upon the bed "fallen sick of his sickness whereof he died." To such a possibility Paul responded, "Most gladly therefore will I rather glory in my infirmities, that the power of Christ may rest upon me" (2 Cor. 12:9). We must conclude that God in His infinite wisdom and love causes "all things [to] work together for good" (Rom. 8:28) in the lives of His own; and sometimes greater blessing or testimony comes from trauma borne in the power of God than would result from healing.

To claim that it is God's will for every Christian to have perfect health is to contradict Hebrews 9:27: "It is appointed unto men once to die." The most spiritual will someday die or get sick on the way, and we will pray about it; but we must leave to God whether or not He sees fit to heal.

D. It Is Proper To Pray for Healing

Far from being wrong to use physicians and medicine, it is to be remembered that in Isaiah 38:1-5 where Hezekiah was healed by God, Isaiah prescribed a fig poultice (38:21). (See also 2 Kings 20:1-11.) A combination of God's power and medicine wrought a miracle. Therefore, pray! The same can be said of Timothy and "a medicinal dose of wine" in 1 Timothy 5:23 and the clay used on the blind man in John 9:1-7.

It is not wise to relegate James 5:13-16 to a previous generation or dispensation and disallow the "prayer of faith." We need to accept it as a simple statement of fact. If a believer "calls for the elders of the church," rather than a professional healer calling for participants in a "healing line"; and if the "elders" are fully persuaded by the Holy Spirit that they should pray for healing, God promises to "save—restore, raise up, forgive and heal." Which method God chooses and the means He employs and the time involved are in God's hands, but it is proper to pray for healing.

However, to claim that healing is in the atonement— available upon demand—is not true. In the truest sense, "every good gift" is ours by way of Jesus Christ and the atonement. Our bodies will one day be perfect; but until then, suffering, sickness and death will remain. See Romans 8:18-23, and pray.

Prepare To Discuss Intelligently

1. List three reasons why we worry.
2. List three reasons why we should not worry.
3. List five verses of Scripture to help us not to worry.
4. List some reasons why people get sick.
5. Cite some Scriptures to help when we pray for the sick.

CHAPTER 12

How To Pray

BIBLE PORTION TO READ: Psalm 95:1-11

THE COMMONALITY of prayer among all men and the common place of prayer in practice reduces it to carelessness on the part of almost everyone. Few sense that we are in the presence of Deity when we pray. Few consider that only properly authorized persons can pray and get results.

When we stop to think about it, we are immediately aware of the fact that if one is not a believer, there is little use in praying. Of course, the matter is compounded if the god to whom one prays does not exist; but even prayer to the one true God is communication between the Heavenly Father and His children. Therefore, aliens, strangers and unbelievers have no basis for expecting God to hear their prayers.

If God does not hear believers who live in sin, how can we expect Him to hear unbelieving sinners? See Isaiah 59:2: "Your iniquities have separated between you and your God, and your sins have hid his face from you, that he will not hear." Like the publican in Luke 18:13, a sinner can pray, "God be merciful to me a sinner"; and, based on Jesus' response to that man, any sinner can be assured that Jesus will hear and forgive and save. On Calvary, the thief cried, "Lord, remember me"; and again Jesus' response warrants the offer of assurance to any who pray thus that they will be heard.

One of the common jokes in our day has to do with do-it-yourself workmen who attempt to make something or assemble something and finally read the book of instructions which was ignored at the outset. Probably most prayer is offered in ignorance of or even in contradiction to the instructions and promises in God's Word. We must know the Word of God so that as we pray, we can pray intelligently and with assurance.

Jesus referred to some whose prayers were "vain repetitions" and others who thought they were heard "for their much speaking." It would appear that the way one prays is important.

I. A Proper Attitude Toward God and Jesus Christ

S. D. Gordon in his classic *Quiet Talks on Prayer* quotes the Lord Jesus as saying in Mark 11:22-24: " 'Have faith in God'—with the emphasis doublelined under the word 'God.' The chief factor in prayer is God. 'Verily I say unto you, whosoever shall say unto this mountain, Be thou taken up and cast into the sea — . . . And shall not doubt in his heart—' That is Jesus' definition of faith. '—But shall believe that what he saith cometh to pass; he shall have it. Therefore, I say unto you, all things whatsoever ye pray and ask for, believe that ye receive them, and ye shall have them.' "

The enormity of these verses can scarcely be imagined! There is no record that Jesus ever asked for a mountain to be moved. He was, however, posing the ultimate impossibility which is surmountable only by prayer. Jesus' evident intent was to place God in the forefront of all our thinking when we pray. There is no use to pray if we do not pray to God. All the faith in the world in other things will produce some things; but when you face impossibilities, only faith in God will work. Only a proper attitude—and that an attitude of faith in God—will suffice when we come to prayer.

Again Gordon quoted our lovely Lord as saying,

"Whatsoever ye shall ask in My name, that will I do, that the Father may be glorified in the Son. If ye shall ask anything in My name, that will I do" (John 14:13, 14). This would seem to put Jesus on a par with His Father when it comes to prayer, and properly so. We must have a proper attitude toward the Lord Jesus Christ when we pray; if we do, nothing is impossible. Certainly we could not expect that one who would insult the Son of God would get anything from God. In John 10:30 Jesus plainly states, "I and my Father are one." The following verses indicate the disbelief of the Jews on the matter of the deity of Christ and the declaration that the works of Jesus Christ prove His oneness with God. This would account for His mountain-moving ability when it comes to prayer. Any uncertainty or disbelief regarding the deity of Christ renders prayer impotent.

Another evidence of the importance of attitudes in prayer is John 15:7: "If ye abide in me, and my words abide in you, ye shall ask what ye will, and it shall be done unto you." If true faith in God and in Jesus Christ will move mountains (the impossible), surely anything else will be no problem to those who just keep on believing—abiding. John 16:23 and 24, our memory verses, put God the Father and Jesus Christ the Son together in the matter of answers to prayer and point up again the importance of a proper personal attitude, that of personal faith and devotion toward God and His Son when we pray.

All of this makes it clear that prayer must be addressed by believers to God through Jesus Christ in an attitude of faith and devotion. There is none of this running into and out of the presence of God, none of this careless rubbing of eyebrows and calling it prayer, none of this inane jibberish called prayer—whether in repeated rote prayers recited minute after minute or in an unintelligible sound called "prayer in the Spirit." Either we enter the place of prayer soberly, reverently and conscious of the person and presence of God, or it is doubtful that what we do can really be called prayer.

II. A Proper Attitude Toward the Word of God

Perhaps it has been true in every dispensation and every generation that unbelievers and worldly believers distort and misapply the truth. For example, in this time, almost no one understands the meaning of "love." A simple study of the words employed would clear things in our minds, but few will take the time to study. Instead, they are caught up in the usage of the moment. *Eros*—erotic, erotica—is a fleshly, sensual, sexual love which is real but has become the only kind of love in the minds of people—saved and unsaved alike. This word is not used in the New Testament.

Hence, if the word *phileo* or *agape* is used, most people have a very erroneous understanding of the love expressed in Scripture because of their preoccupation with erotic love. In John 3:16 we have, "God so loved" *(agape);* and in Titus 2:4 we read, "Young women . . . to love [*philos*] their husbands, to love [*philos*] their children"; but these are not understood. In these latter instances the word "love—*agape*" is the divine, sacrificial, absolute love of God, or the "love—*philos*" of tender affection, esteem and unselfishness which can be exhibited between any two people and be pure and proper. The world has so distorted the word "love" because of the ignorance of God's Word that they effectively destroy the Word of God. A classic illustration is the travesty—even blasphemy—of the love of Jesus Christ portrayed in the rock-opera film "Jesus Christ Superstar."

Virtually the same thing has happened to the word "faith." Any kind of respect, belief, confidence or credence in anything or anyone is accepted as a valid expression of Biblical faith. Ecumenism accepts as valid the simple statement, "I believe in God," whether or not Jesus Christ is considered to be the divine Son of God. Any practice employed by anyone who calls himself a Christian is accepted. The confusion in music used in worship, the dress or undress tolerated, the language—reverent or profane—used is acceptable if the person involved professes "faith" in Jesus.

You may wonder what this has to do with our subject, "How To Pray." The connection is in the fact that "not everyone that saith . . . Lord, Lord" is really a Christian. Not everyone who stands with one finger raised toward Heaven, swaying rhythmically from side to side, chanting "I love Jesus" is a Christian. Not everyone who kneels, stands, raises his hand and piously "prays" is really a Christian; and for the sake of the souls of men, someone had better remind them, "To the law and to the testimony: if they speak not according to this word, it is because there is no light in them" (Isa. 8:20). Someone needs to warn that God is not pleased to accept any kind of a gesture or expression titled faith as a basis for salvation or for prayer. Jesus said, "I am the way, the truth, and the life: no man cometh unto the Father, but by me" (John 14:6). We are also reminded in Acts 4:12: "There is none other name under heaven given among men, whereby we must be saved."

Someone needs to remind us that we must accept the truth declared in the Word of God, the promises of the Word of God and the words of the Word of God in a proper, intelligent way or we may be unsaved and helpless in prayer. We cannot know how to be saved unless we know and believe the Word of God. We cannot know how to pray unless we know, believe and claim the promises of God's Word. Anytime a person can support his faith or practice by clear statements of Scripture, he is on sound foundation and can expect to be successful. The converse is also true; unless the faith and practice can be supported with Scripture, there is danger of building upon sand. "So then faith cometh by hearing, and hearing by the word of God" (Rom. 10:17).

Search the Bible; read the promises; mark them; memorize them and claim them as you pray. No wonder the Devil spends so much time denying, questioning, challenging, perverting and even paraphrasing the Word of God!

Such attention—and such an attitude toward the Word of God—will give the Holy Spirit opportunity to apply His purifying power to our lives and give confidence as we pray. In 1 John 3:22 we read, "And whatsoever we ask, we receive of him, because we keep his commandments, and do those things that are pleasing in his sight."

Dr. John R. Rice urges, "Act upon the faith you have." Hebrews 11:6 declares that we must have faith but also that we must act on our faith, be it new or old, large or small. We must "not only believe that he is" but "diligently seek him." Perhaps the list of the heroes of faith in this chapter will encourage us to find out what God has said and then do what God asks without worrying too much about the manifold ramifications of faith and prayer. Each of us can and should emulate personally these men imperishably memorialized in God's Hall of Faith—Hebrews 11.

We do not know or read the promises made by God in every case; but we know that all of these—and the rest in Hebrews 11—had a promise or promises that led them to action, which action resulted in their enshrinement as heroes unto God. We are to go and do likewise. "Search the Scriptures," and act upon the promises God gives to validate your prayers.

III. Proper Attitudes When We Pray

A. In *Quiet Talks on Prayer* S. D. Gordon confirms our efforts in this lesson by saying, "The first thing in prayer is to find God's purpose, the trend, the swing of it." Does it sound strange for this great man to speak thus? He was saying just what we have tried to say; namely, become personally acquainted with God and His dear Son. Then walk so closely with Him that prayer becomes conversation with our Heavenly Father. "The second thing [is] to make that purpose our prayer. We want to find out what God is thinking, and then to claim that that shall be done." We have urged exploring God's Word so that we may know the will of God and then pray about what God wants and promises.

Perhaps some will consider a discussion of the mechanics of prayer unnecessary and even unwise. But to this author it seems that our attitudes toward God and His words result in certain physical attitudes when we pray. True, ejaculatory prayers may be the spontaneous, unrehearsed, informal prayers spawned in a moment or in an emergency; but this does not legitimatize the irreverent informality that is so common and even recommended these days.

If there is protocol for dress and behavior in the presence of a monarch or a President; if there is etiquette for weddings, banquets and church services; ought there not to be a proper way to pray? We realize that each of these areas is treated with utmost informality these days, but that does not make it right. It would not be difficult to make a case against this "neo" approach to Scripture, morality, propriety, dress, etc. Whether this approach is the cause or the result may be debatable, but the effect certainly is questionable.

S. D. Gordon also suggests that we need a "trysting place." A time and place to meet God is a most valuable assist to prayer. Neither the time nor place is technically significant since any hour and any location can be that chink in the wall or refuge where we can meet to commune with God and make our requests known. "Come, my people, enter thou into thy chambers, and shut thy doors about thee: hide thyself as it were for a little moment" (Isa. 26:20). And Matthew 6:6 reads, "When thou prayest, enter into thy closet, and when thou hast shut thy door, pray."

B. Gordon also suggests that we "give the Book of God its place in prayer." Reading the Word is the listening part of prayer. "The purpose of God comes in through the ear, passes through the heart taking on the tinge of your personality, and goes out at the tongue as prayer." It is proper and helpful to ask the Holy Spirit to guide us into all truth and lead us in our prayers, since these are some of His responsibilities (John 16:13; Rom. 8:26). Gordon has gone so far as to suggest that "the highest law of the Christian life is obedience to the leading of the Holy Spirit. . . . He should be allowed to . . . dominate our praying. . . . It will take time . . . if you will just yield and patiently wait, He will teach what to pray, suggest definite things, and often the very language of prayer." "Rest in the LORD, and wait patiently for him" (Ps. 37:7).

C. "Prayer must be in Jesus' name." Again back to our memory verses to remind us of the importance of knowing Jesus Christ, trusting Him and consciously approaching God as His child because you have been born again. The idle use of the phrase, "In Jesus' name, Amen," with which we close our prayers is not the intent of this suggestion. Again we must remind that it takes time, quietness and perhaps reading the Word to be sure that we are conscious of our entrance into the presence of God, accomplished through Jesus Christ. Meditation on the presence of Christ at the mercy seat (Heb. 7:25) will put us in the proper attitude. It is then that Jesus—and I speak reverently—takes us by the hand into the presence of God and says, "Father, let Me introduce My friend." Be sure to remind God that you came in "the Name." Also it reminds Satan that he must loosen his clutches and leave you alone while you pray.

D. To all of this, we add some proper attitudes in prayer practiced by Bible pray-ers:

1. Kneeling is enjoined in Psalm 95:6. Read the admonition in Isaiah 45:22-25. Of course, this has to do with other than prayer; but if kneeling is required of all—willing or unwilling—ought it not be the habit of true believers?

In 1 Kings 8:54, Solomon rose from kneeling on his knees in prayer; and in 2 Chronicles 6:13, Solomon "stood, and kneeled down upon his knees . . . and spread forth his hands toward heaven" and prayed.

In Ezra 9:5 we read that Ezra fell upon his knees, and spread out his hands unto the Lord God and prayed.

In Daniel 6:10 Daniel "went into his house; and his windows being open in his chamber toward Jerusalem, he kneeled upon his knees three times a day."

Jesus withdrew "from them about a stone's cast, and kneeled down, and prayed" (Luke 22:41).

Stephen, in Acts 7:60, "kneeled down, and cried with a loud voice."

Peter (Acts 9:40) "put them all forth, and kneeled down, and prayed."

Paul (Acts 20:36) "kneeled down, and prayed with them all"—the Ephesian elders—and again in Acts 21:5, with another group of believers, "we kneeled down on the shore, and prayed."

And read Paul's words in Ephesians 3:14.

There may be better ways to pray, but I choose to be in the company of such men as these and in such an attitude as to reflect humility in God's presence. Probably no other physical attitude is so often practiced, recommended and effective.

2. In Numbers 20:6 Moses and Aaron "fell upon their faces: and the glory of the LORD appeared unto them." "And Joshua fell on his face to the earth, and did worship" (Josh. 5:14). Elijah in 1 Kings 18:42 and Jehoshaphat in 2 Chronicles 20:18 similarly prostrated

themselves before God, and their prayers were heard. In Gethsemane Jesus "fell on his face, and prayed" (Matt. 26:39), revealing to us that this attitude is usually used in intense moments of anguish or need.

3. Standing as we pray is also a recommended attitude and practice as in 1 Kings 8:22 where Solomon "stood before the altar of the LORD . . . and spread forth his hands toward heaven." Jesus even exhorted, "And when ye stand praying, forgive" (Mark 11:25). In Luke 18 we have the account of the Pharisee and the publican in prayer. Both stood praying (vv. 11, 13); therefore, the difference in the results indicates that standing, kneeling and prostration are not guarantees that prayer will be heard. Rather, the humility and faith with which we pray are the determining factors. The incident indicates that the attitude of stillness and reverence is expected anytime we pray.

It is scarcely possible to overestimate the importance of our attitudes when we talk about how to pray. We must have an attitude of reverence toward God and faith in Jesus Christ. We also must have confidence in God's Word and its promises and be respectful and humble in posture.

Prepare To Discuss Intelligently

1. What is a proper attitude toward God if we expect answers to prayer?

2. What is a necessary attitude toward the Bible in the matter of prayer? Why?

3. Which posture in prayer do you consider best? Why?

4. What additional attitudes or postures would you suggest?

Source of Quotations

Gordon, S. D. *Quiet Talks on Prayer*. Old Tappan, NJ: Fleming H. Revell Co., 1904, pp. 130, 148, 150, 152, 154, 155. Used by permission.

CHAPTER 13

Promises! Promises! Promises!

BIBLE PORTION TO READ: Psalm 84:1-12

NORMAN B. HARRISON in *His in a Life of Prayer* stated, "It remains for us to see that God's provision for a Life of Prayer is an all-comprehensive 'coverage'; that by it He proposes to care for every necessity, every exigency of our earthly existence, as it may arise."

In *Philippians 4:6* Paul wrote, "Be careful for nothing"; literally, do not allow yourself to be pulled apart, pulled in two directions, filled full with care, concern, worry, conviction, anything or nothing. God has a remedy, a solution and a way to handle it—no matter what it is! It is the way of prayer! "Every thing by prayer," said Paul, although he added for emphasis "by . . . supplication and thanksgiving."

It appears that Paul was urging a bold, businesslike, persistent, persuasive campaign in prayer which would include simple requests, petitions or desires. It also included deep, repeated imploring and pleading. It suggests stopping every now and then to appraise the situation and to give thanks for answers—even partial answers—and then go on. It would seem that the exhortation of Jesus in Luke 18:1, "Men ought always [allways] to pray, and not to faint [or give up or grow weary or discouraged]" is the same thing.

The inescapable conviction which comes from the reading of Scripture is that every contingency in human experience is covered by prayer. Further, there is a promise in God's Word to cover any and every type of need, even though the words or names may have changed. The door to the prayer closet is never locked.

The promise given in the memory verses is literally: peace over and above anything man can give and beyond what men can explain or even understand. That God can see and hear and answer prayer should be no problem for those of us who have seen and heard the transmission of sound and pictures around the world in an instant of time, and from the earth to the moon and back in a few seconds. If man can direct the flight of a spaceship from a console in a concrete blockhouse in Texas, should it be thought strange that the omnipotent, sovereign God of the universe should hear and answer prayer? When word of news happenings all around the world are relayed to us in minutes, should we question God's ability to touch the lives of His children and give them peace about anything they ask Him?

It is worth noting that the memory verses promise that "peace . . . shall keep [garrison, guard] your hearts and minds [as with a military guard or within a secured place] through Christ." It is an evil anomaly, irregularity and even contradiction that so many who read and quote Philippians 4:6 consume as much aspirin and as many tranquilizers as those who do not know God and do not know how to pray. Is there within us an "evil heart of unbelief" that prevents us from praying and/or defeats us when we pray, because we fail to make all our requests known or fail to cast all our care upon Him or insist on worrying even in the place of guarded protection and sure supply?

Look up and read Cleland McAfee's song: "There is a place of quiet rest, near to the heart of God."

Many have taken in hand to set in order the abundance of promises concerning prayer contained in

God's Word. Our effort, therefore, is not new or even different; but our intention is to provide an index of prayer promises in the hope that it may provide encouragement to prayer and stimulation in prayer.

I. General Prayer Promises

Read Isaiah 40:31. Do we have any idea what this verse means? We understand the words; most of us have experimented with the offer of prayer contained in the word "wait"; but have we tried to walk in the strength God promises when we have none of our own? Have we tried to get above the circumstances on those eagles' wings? Have we run or walked far beyond our ability because we were His very own and we were on business for the King? Or have we slumped dejectedly in our weariness and prayed for a miracle to occur to get us out of our dilemma? Perhaps we ran quickly for a tranquilizer because "these things always bring on a headache." Or we disconsolately, resignedly sat down to wait for things to change, accepting perhaps that "all things work together for good," but getting no victory, no joy out of our situation and adding little, if anything, to our testimony for Christ.

Psalm 37:4, 5: "Delight thyself also in the LORD." This sounds like Matthew 6:33. A valid, viable faith and a genuine endeavor at doing the will of God are prerequisites for victory and success in any endeavor on the part of a believer. Now the verse says, "Delight thyself." In other words, we are to take pleasure in, participate in, get enthusiastic about, act as if we enjoy being an "in the LORD" person! Too much of the time we act as if we were sorry God saved us and are burdened by the effort to live Christian lives. Think of James 1:7. Let's get out of this crabby, complaining, hypocritical false piety and false modesty and begin to delight ourselves in the pursuit of godliness! I'd rather be a saved slave or a sanctified pauper or an indwelt invalid than to be lost, unsaved, but rich and famous. Would you?

Let's continue reading *Psalm 37:4 and 5*. Doesn't that sound like Proverbs 3:5 and 6? (Read these verses too.) This is speaking of the matter of faith followed by works, faith followed by obedience, faith augmented by diligent effort to walk worthy of the calling to be saints—sons of God, who walk in light, love, circumspectly, not as unbelievers walk (Eph. 4:1, 17; 5:2, 8, 15). This is a matter of such great importance that none should miss it. Yet many presume that once one has said, "Lord, I believe; help Thou my unbelief," the only thing he needs to do is sit idly by and do what comes naturally. Then we wonder why we have no power in prayer or effectiveness in testimony.

Take time to read the additional precious promises in Isaiah 41:10; Philippians 4:13 and Psalm 37:23 and 24.

II. Promises Relative to Salvation

Think upon *Isaiah 55:6, 7:* "Seek ye the LORD while he may be found, call ye upon him while he is near: let the wicked forsake his way, and the unrighteous man his thoughts: and let him return unto the LORD, and he will have mercy upon him; and to our God, for he will abundantly pardon."

Consider *Romans 10:9, 10, 13:* "That if thou shalt confess with thy mouth the Lord Jesus, and shalt believe in thine heart that God hath raised him from the dead, thou shalt be saved. For with the heart man believeth unto righteousness; and with the mouth confession is made unto salvation. . . . For whosoever shall call upon the name of the Lord [Jesus Christ] shall be saved."

These verses from both Old and New Testaments make it clear that God's provision for saving men is available to sinful men by their seeking, believing, confessing and calling. The example of the publican whose prayer was simply a prayer for mercy (Luke 18:13) and that of the thief on the cross who prayed, "Lord, remember me" (Luke 23:42), give credence to the remark by Dr. James M. Gray, former president of the Moody Bible Institute: "God is so completely satisfied with the work of His Son that He will accept as valid the least pretense of faith." It is our joy to be able to tell men everywhere that "God so loved" (John 3: 16) that "whosoever believeth in him should not perish, but have everlasting life." We can assure men: "Forasmuch as ye know that ye were not redeemed with corruptible things, as silver and gold, from your vain conversation . . . but with the precious blood of Christ, as of a lamb without blemish and without spot . . . foreordained before the foundation of the world, but was manifest in these last times for you" (1 Pet. 1:18-20).

On the other hand, Peter urged in *2 Peter 1:10 and 11:* "Give diligence to make your calling and election sure . . . for so an entrance shall be ministered unto you abundantly into the everlasting kingdom of our Lord and Saviour Jesus Christ." Let none subscribe to the "easy-believism" of our day which makes it appear that anything vaguely resembling faith will work; nor to the legalism which adds to the Word of God baptism, a second work of grace or anything else. Let us make diligent application of the promises of Acts 16:31; John 1:12 and 5:24, confirming the promises with evidence observable and genuine.

III. Promises Relative to Assurance or Guidance

Since believers still live on earth in bodies of flesh,

and since we have an enemy who "as a roaring lion, walketh about, seeking whom he may devour" (1 Pet. 5:8), the tactics that worked in the Garden of Eden are still employed. The result is that unless we are careful to maintain the attitude of 1 John 2:15-17: "Love not the world, neither the things that are in the world," the first thing we know, we will have fallen into sin.

To say that one has no sin is to be a lying hypocrite (1 John 1:10), but we have the promise of 1 John 1:9: "If we confess our sins, he [Who saved us] is faithful and just to forgive us our sins, and to cleanse us from all unrighteousness." Far from losing our salvation and getting saved all over again and again, the blood which cleanses all our sins is applied to the sins now confessed by the believer.

Our every appearance at the Lord's Table is another opportunity thus to confess our sins as we hear, "This is my blood of the new testament, which is shed for many for the remission of sins" (Matt. 26:28).

Sometimes we find ourselves afraid, uncertain and doubting. Often it is because we are ignorant of what God may be doing or unsure of His leading. Then we need to hear *Jeremiah 33:3:* "Call unto me, and I will answer thee, and shew thee great and mighty things, which thou knowest not," or *Psalm 56:3:* "What time I am afraid, I will trust in thee," or *Psalm 37:23:* "The steps of a good man are ordered by the LORD." Someone has commented that this also involves the "stops" of a good man.

In *Isaiah 30:19-21* what is addressed to Israel is applicable to fearful believers today: "He will be very gracious unto thee at the voice of thy cry [prayer]; when he shall hear it, he will answer thee. . . . And thine ears shall hear a word behind thee, saying, This is the way, walk ye in it, when ye turn to the right hand, and when ye turn to the left."

James 1:5 has long been a favorite when uncertainties or problems create concern: "If any of you lack wisdom, let him ask of God, that giveth to all men liberally, and upbraideth not; and it shall be given him." Often we will lie or bluff or have something to say rather than be thought ignorant. The wise man honestly admits his ignorance and diligently seeks an answer. If it were possible to wear out a passage of Scripture, this author would have done so with James 1:5. Countless times this verse has been called to the attention of the Heavenly Father with a new set of names or details inserted and a plea for wisdom to meet the need. James 1:5 seems to offer a man the opportunity to seek of God the wisdom, strength and courage to resolve a problem or meet a need in a manner that gives one the gratification of having worked with God. *Philippians 4:13* fits here too: "I can do all things through Christ which strengtheneth me."

IV. Promises Regarding Adversity or Temptation

Psalm 50:15: "And call upon me in the day of trouble: I will deliver thee, and thou shalt glorify me."

Psalm 91:15, 16: "He shall call upon me, and I will answer him: I will be with him in trouble; I will deliver him, and honour him. With long life will I satisfy him, and shew him my salvation."

Psalm 55:22: "Cast thy burden upon the LORD, and he shall sustain thee."

First Peter 5:7: "Casting all your care upon him; for he careth for you." Someone has written:

> "Bear not a single care thyself.
> One is too much for thee.
> The work is Mine and Mine alone;
> Thy work to trust in Me."

Each of the above verses make the same promise. Too much of the time our needs, problems, adversities and those of our friends dominate our prayers. How many times God must wait while we pray—even in church prayer meetings—to hear one request that is solely a spiritual matter! We hear requests for money, illness, jobs, wants and needs but seldom a prayer for souls and only occasionally a prayer for the pastor and his spiritual ministry.

First Corinthians 10:13: "There hath no temptation [testing, trial] taken you but such as is common to man." The temptation here is not primarily a temptation to sin but rather a testing or trial. However, in either case the promise is that God will not let it break us down. As in the case of Job, there are limitations which God imposes since His purpose is to build us up, not tear us down; to demonstrate our strength, not illustrate our weakness; to encourage dependence on Him, not expose us to peril, sin and defeat. Also, the Lord promises "a way to escape" which the following phrase indicates to be a way through the test rather than an escape from it or a way around it. Like David, we walk "through the valley of the shadow" and every other dark place. We do not cower or collapse because we have the promise, "As thy days, so shall thy strength be" (Deut. 33:25). See also *Psalm 84:5, 7 and 8:* "Blessed is the man whose strength is in thee. . . . They go from strength to strength. . . . O LORD God of hosts, hear my prayer."

There is virtually no end to the promises along this line. We only add a few: Job 5:19; 2 Timothy 4:18; 2 Peter 2:9; Isaiah 46:4; Jeremiah 1:8; 2 Corinthians 1: 10; 1 Peter 3:12; Deuteronomy 20:4; Proverbs 2:8 and Hebrews 13:5. Take time to read each one.

V. Promises Regarding Spiritual Life and Revival

Psalm 126:5, 6: "They that sow [pray] in tears shall reap in joy. He that goeth forth and weepeth, bearing precious seed, shall doubtless come again with rejoicing, bringing his sheaves with him." The tendency to lethargy and Laodicean lukewarmness should stir us to prayer. Nothing will so stimulate prayer as much as a burden for souls. May our prayer be that of *Psalm 85:6 and 7:* "Wilt thou not revive us again: that thy people may rejoice in thee? Shew us thy mercy, O

LORD, and grant us thy salvation."

We need to be reminded that God "will have all men to be saved, and to come unto the knowledge of the truth" (1 Tim. 2:4). Also *2 Peter 3:9* holds encouragement for us: "The Lord is not slack concerning his promise [concerning prayer, the Second Coming, salvation] . . . but is longsuffering to us-ward, not willing that any should perish, but that all should come to repentance." Keep praying for the lost with the assurance that it will both win them to Christ and preserve your spiritual life.

Promises! Promises! Promises! The Word of God is full of them. There are promises upon which we pray and promises made if and when we pray. Make diligent search for promises which—if claimed—will build you up in godliness, encourage and bless you and others and result in salvation of the lost and glory to God.

Prepare To Discuss Intelligently

1. Write down your favorite prayer promise.
2. Relate Isaiah 41:10 and 1 Corinthians 10:13.
3. Have you ever claimed James 1:5? For what?
4. Explain 1 Corinthians 10:13, especially the word "temptation."
5. Write down 1 Timothy 2:4.

CHAPTER 14

The Lord's Prayer

BIBLE PORTION TO READ: John 17:1-26

OUR GREAT HIGH PRIEST appeared on the eve of the offering of Himself as the Sacrifice for His people. With divine prescience He saw the whole mystery of the cross, the grave, the Resurrection and the Ascension as already achieved. One of the great mysteries of inspiration is how John succeeded in recording this prayer word for word. However, Jesus expected such things would happen and guaranteed an accurate record in John 14:25 and 26. (Take time to read the verses.)

One must take off his shoes as he walks up the slopes of Mount Moriah while this Isaac talks with His Father on the way to the place of sacrifice. This Isaac knew He was the Lamb of God, but no trace of fear appeared in this divine discourse.

Keep this prayer in mind when we later go into Gethsemane so we can balance the agony of *that* hour with the cool confidence of *this* hour. The years of looking toward Calvary now began to compress themselves into a few days and hours. Having extended the hope of John 14:1-6 and the promise of the Comforter in the verses which followed, He spoke the words of John 14: 27-30.

I. Christ's Personal Prayer (John 17:1-5)

It is not really important where this prayer was prayed. It does not appear that it was in Gethsemane but somewhere between the upper room—where Jesus probably uttered the words of John 14—and the Garden. Would it be wrong to presume that He took the disciples to the Temple area, discoursed on the vine and the branches (John 15) and their future Director, viz., the Holy Spirit, as they sat thus with Jerusalem spread out before them (John 16)? Then, as dusk began to fall, He began to pray as recorded for us here in John 17.

Verse 1 of the next chapter would seem to indicate that it was *after* this prayer that Jesus and the disciples went over Kidron and into "a place called Gethsemane" (Matt. 26:36; John 18:1). It blesses my soul to imagine such a scene; and it stills my heart as I reverently bow my head and listen while the Son of God prays, "Glorify thy Son."

A. The condition was complete and open fellowship. Note that Jesus, with proper deference to the position and authority of the Father, addressed Himself not to "the Father" or "My Father"; but as a servant to a master simply as "Father." All else in these first five verses emphasized Christ's voluntary humility as He used such phrases as "thy Son"; "given him power"; "as many as thou hast given him"; "I have finished the work which thou gavest me to do." If the Son of God entered God's presence with such complete humility and subjection, ought we not do likewise when we pray? How dare we come to God like an impudent child acting as though we had a claim on God's attention and response? Too much of our praying is devoid of this kind of respect and reverential awe.

B. Note also that Jesus fully recognized this relationship with the Father: "thy Son"; "Jesus Christ, whom thou hast sent"; and "the glory which I had with thee before the world was." The "conscious divinity of the Son," as Alexander Maclaren referred to it, was very evident. Just as the "Logos" in John 1:1, 14 and 18 was declared, so here it was confirmed by the Logos Himself. Just as "he that hath seen me hath seen the Father" (John 14:9), so here His unique nature was affirmed. Compare Philippians 2:5-11 and 1 Timothy 3:16 with the declaration here. Jesus was aware of the mystery of the Incarnation and divine Sonship, and He sought confirmation of it in the concluding scenes about to be portrayed. Certainly these statements establish the relationship of the divine-human Christ beyond question and provide another basis for prayer. We must be able to kneel upon the foundation of Sonship with God when we pray, "Abba, Father." Is your praying founded upon a personal relationship with God through faith in Jesus Christ (Gal. 4:6)?

C. Then comes the petition "glorify," requested two times (vv. 1 and 5). The word "glorify" basically means "to form an opinion," which in verse 1 is tantamount to the petition that God confirms the testimony that Jesus had borne during the three years of His earthly ministry. "I have glorified thee on the earth: I have finished the work which thou gavest me to do," said Jesus. He had spoken words; He had performed works; He had spoken of the promised "eternal life" to as many as received Him, the same ones "which thou gavest me [Him]." Incidentally, notice that seven times Jesus spoke of believers as being given to Him by the Father (vv. 2, 6, 9, 11, 12, 24—see Scofield's note on John 17:2).

119

The conflict, combat, death and resurrection would prove God's love and the truth of all Jesus had said about Himself, God and the nature of eternal life. Thus He would glorify God in the "hour" now come and the "hour" about which He prayed in Gethsemane. Any failure now, any Satanic success now would frustrate the divine plan and deprive God of the glory inherent in the victory of the cross and the tomb. The awfulness of Gethsemane is seen when it is held up against the pure light of this petition. This prayer is not for any selfish glory, but for the glory of God in the confirmation of everything revealed from Eden by Moses, the Prophets, the Psalms and the Gospels.

Let us digress a moment to consider the "life eternal" to which Jesus referred in John 17:3. To quote the *Pulpit Commentary:* "This 'life' . . . is clearly more than, and profoundly different from, the principle of unending existence. Life is more than perpetuity of being, and eternity is not endlessness, nor is 'eternal life' a mere prolongation of duration; it refers rather to state and quality than to one condition of that state; it is the negation of time rather than indefinite or infinite prolongation of time. That which Christ gives to those who believe in Him, receive Him, is the life of God Himself." It is further described as "a present realizable possession" which in nowise minimizes the future aspects of the glory which is yet to come. Look up Matthew 19:29; Mark 10:30 and Luke 18:30 where the practice of the life of faith in this world is seen as a prelude to more of the same throughout the ages to come. Doubtless something of this concept is contained in Paul's comment, "Eye hath not seen" (1 Cor. 2:9). Think of it if you dare! Jesus has given eternal life to us because God is glorified when we who believe live as the children of God here and now on the way to Heaven!

Here is another thought: Does your life glorify God? Does your praying glorify God? To pray as Jesus did, we must have that relationship with God and maintain that fellowship with God which seeks nothing more or less than the glory and praise of God. How puerile most of our praying must seem to God! Before Jesus could resume the glory which He had "before the world was," He must do all God gave Him to do. May we not conclude that before we assume the glory prepared for and reserved for us, we, too, ought to glorify God in all that He planned in Ephesians 2:10?

II. Christ's Prayer for His Disciples (John 17:6-19)

Before we look at the petitions our Lord made for the disciples, let us look at characteristics of the disciples here described. Perhaps these features are limited exclusively to the Twelve—about to be reduced to eleven—but I think not. It seems more likely that any true disciple of Jesus Christ would be possessed of these same characteristics.

A. "They have kept thy word" (v. 6). Note also verse 8. These men had been fully exposed to the person of God, the deity of the Son and the Messiahship of Jesus Christ, as well as the Lordship of Christ. Whether this manifestation had come "when he opened to us [them] the scriptures," or in those intimate conversations of which there must have been many, they had become convinced, convicted believers.

B. Not only had the disciples received, believed and accepted the revelation conveyed to them in the person of Jesus Christ—received His Word—but "they have kept thy word." In verse 6 the "word" is *logos* and most certainly is connected with "thy name" in the same verse, and with the "Word"—*logos* in John 1:1 and 14. These men received the person of God as well as the truth of God revealed in Jesus Christ. Now in verse 8 where we read "they have received them" [the words], it is another term, *raymata,* denoting that which is spoken. These "words" have directed them to faith. These "words" have convinced them that "I came out from thee . . . and thou didst send me."

Is there any possibility that we could overstate the

121

necessity for knowing the Word of God, believing the Word of God and receiving the Word of God, both in its personal manifestation *(Logos)* in Jesus Christ or in its inscription *(raymata)* in Holy Writ? I think not! "They have kept thy word" means "to keep an eye on, watch over or preserve," which only emphasizes the need for attending to and studying God's Word and His words. The very word "disciples" goes beyond mere believing to serious study.

C. Another characteristic is given in verse 14. There is an unworldliness that engenders opposition, misunderstanding and even hatred and persecution. Again to quote the *Pulpit Commentary:* "This constant contrast between the mind of Christ and the spirit of the world pervades the New Testament. Christ had exposed its hypocrisies, and denounced its idols, and inverted its standards, and repudiated its smile [approbation], and condemned its price [and its sin], and was now indifferent to its curse. His disciples, as far as they shared His sentiments, came in also for its malediction and hatred."

Is it not a strange anomaly in our day that so few of the disciples of our Lord are distinguishable from the world, to say nothing of being "un-hated" by the world? Have we become so completely lukewarm that the world is comfortable around us, and are we more concerned about the approbation of the world than identification as His disciples? Could this have anything to do with our impotence in prayer? In witnessing? In winning the lost?

When we come now to the prayer of our Lord for the disciples, note several details in verses 6-19:

1. He prayed for them personally (v. 9). "I pray for them . . . not for the world." This is a very emphatic way of demonstrating His concern for the disciples, and it is not to be interpreted as any lack of concern for the world. There is no contradiction between this statement and those which enjoin us to pray "for them which despitefully use you" (Matt. 5:44), or "for all

men; for kings, and for all that are in authority" (1 Tim. 2:1, 2), etc. This is in no sense in conflict with "God so loved the world" (John 3:16) or "the Lamb of God, which taketh away the sin of the world" (John 1:29). This is simply a very powerful, personal prayer for His very special disciples.

2. The key portion of this prayer is here in the word-"keep" (vv. 11, 15). There are two words employed here and in verse 12. One word *tayreo* we have already noted in verse 6. This word means "to give attention to, to keep an eye on, watch over, preserve" and suggests personal attention. The other word *phulasso* means "to guard, protect, fence in, set a watch" and is a military-type word which emphasizes the security involved. In verses 6, 11 and 15 the former word is used. Hence, whether it be the disciples or God, the idea is personal preservation or attention. For this Jesus pleads in remarkable words, "Holy Father, keep"! Does it not thrill your soul to hear Jesus ask God to keep an eye on His disciples? Does it not excite you to be a disciple when you realize that it brings you into this kind of relationship with God?

In verse 12 Jesus remarked that while He was with the disciples in the world, He both "kept an eye on them" *(tayreo)* and "guarded them" *(phulasso)*. No problem is created by the fact that "none of them is lost, but the son of perdition"; for we recognize that Judas' defection was foreseen in Psalm 41:9 and quoted by the Lord Jesus in John 13:18. However, now that Jesus was not going to be with His disciples, He committed their care and protection to His Father.

A very interesting view of verse 15 makes Jesus' prayer to read, "I pray not that thou shouldest take them out of the world, but that thou shouldest keep them from the evil [one]." In the Lord's Prayer in Matthew 6:13, the clause "deliver us from evil" differs from this clause "keep them from the evil" in that a different preposition is used. *Apo* is used in Matthew 6 and *ek* in John 17. The distinction is that the former means "away from" while the latter means "out of, or out from inside." This latter usage is felt by most commentators, including Luther and Calvin, to mean protection from the Evil One. How we need such protection!

Another interesting aspect of this verse stems from the remark, "I pray not that thou shouldest take them out of the world." It is usually agreed that it is not God's purpose to take His children out of or away from temptation, the attack of the Evil One or testing and trial. God usually chooses to provide "a way to escape" by giving grace or strength or assistance or comfort so that we are able to "mount up with wings as eagles" (Isa. 40:31) or pass "through the valley of Baca." We are to exhibit Christ in our lives in the marketplace, behind the counter, among the people "that they may see your good works, and glorify your Father" (Matt. 5:16). The Rev. B. Thomas in the *Pulpit Commentary* explained that Jesus did not ask God to take the disciples out of the world but rather to protect them in the world because (1) "They had not yet completed their earthly education" in the school of the Comforter. (2) They had much work to do for Christ when He would commission them in Matthew 28:19 and 20. (3) The earth had need of their "salt" and "light," and Heaven was not yet ready for them (John 14:1-3).

3. A final petition in this prayer for the disciples is in verse 17: "Sanctify them." Much misunderstanding exists about sanctification which Jesus removes by using the word *hagiasmos* rather than *katharizo*, the former meaning "separation from evil and separation unto God" as compared to the latter which means "cleanse, purify, free from impurity or make holy." This, of course, fits with our Lord's petition not to take His disciples out of the world but rather to set them apart for the work whereunto He had called them. (See John 15:15-19.)

III. Our Lord's Prayer for Believers (John 17:20-26)

Space and time are about to forsake us as we come to this wonderful portion of our Lord's Prayer in which "them also which shall believe on me through their word [the disciples' word]" are included. We are those for whom He prayed, and the three petitions uttered in our behalf are tremendous.

A. That they may be one—the prayer for unity (vv. 21-23). The unity here petitioned seems clearly to mean that oneness of nature described by the words "born of the Spirit" (John 3:6), resulting in eternal life and the transformation described by Paul as "a new creature" (2 Cor. 5:17).

In verse 22 the oneness is "even as we are one," prefaced by reference to "the glory which thou gavest me." The glory of open-faced fellowship with God, boldness in the presence of God and access to the throne of grace are here prayed for; and all who enjoy this precious fellowship say, "Thank You, Lord." See 1 John 1:1-4.

In verse 23 note the unity "in" glory as well as "of" glory: "made perfect in one." We will be completely and perfectly one in Christ and with Christ.

So far there is not the slightest hint of what we know as ecumenism. Jesus Christ was praying for every believer, but the emphasis is personal and singular.

B. Christ prayed that the world may believe—the prayer for effective testimony (vv. 21, 23). In verse 21 we read that a regenerated sinner, a transformed life, will convince the world that God loves and is able to save. It will make the gospel understandable by practical illustrations rnultiplied a thousand times. It will make theology a living body of truth as it is seen to work in every aspect of the lives of those who are "believing through their word."

Further, in verse 23 the glory in Jesus Christ's face seen in the faces of believers will cause the world to "know that thou hast sent me, and hast loved them, as thou hast loved me." Each individual believer, according to his capacity, filling his place in the Body of Christ causes the world to come to know through faith and experience what they need most; viz., the love and knowledge of God.

"It is impossible to exclude from these verses," says the *Pulpit Commentary,* "the idea of the *visibility* of the union and life of the Church" in a visible form. "Christians are not, by reason of their differences, to exclude from this passage the promises that the whole assembly of the Firstborn would make this gracious and convincing impression on the world . . . but they have no right to import into the words, by reason of their predilection for particular forms of Church organization, any identification of the body of Christ with any specific form" (denomination) or collective unity (ecumenicity). Ultimately this prayer will be answered; meanwhile, the demonstration of our spiritual oneness is pretty much a personal, sometimes a local church demonstration.

C. The final petition is, "I will that they . . . be with me where I am . . . that they may behold my glory." Read Titus 2:13 and 1 Thessalonians 4:16 and 17. Let us earnestly pray, "Even so, come, Lord Jesus" (Rev. 22:20).

Prepare To Discuss Intelligently

1. Cite the threefold division of John 17 according to the objects of Christ's prayer.

2. What two conditions for effective prayer are illustrated by Christ here in John 17?

3. Give the two meanings of the word "keep" used in this prayer.

4. Define "sanctify" in two ways. Which way is used here?

5. Discuss the unity for which Christ prayed and the unity sought by the ecumenists.